The CCPA Compliance

California's Path to Consumer Privacy

DV Dronamraju

Table of Contents

Free the world of data breaches

About this book

California Consumer Privacy Act (CCPA) provides privacy rights and consumer protection for California residents. Officially called AB-375, Governor Jerry Brown signed this into law on June 28, 2018. Most businesses dealing with personal information of California residents have to comply with this law. Your compliance plan needs to be in place and ready on Jan 1, 2020. This book is designed to help executives think differently about privacy and become a data-driven organization.

For those who already understand GDPR and are already in compliance (GDPR compliance), this book may help you find ways to leverage your earlier investment. It is also designed to focus on data ethics, and the purpose of data collection. By reading or reviewing this book, you will be able to design a new path to privacy in your organization and address the following questions:

- If your customer data is the product, should you rethink a new future?
- Should you spend money on compliance or pay the penalties?
- How do you use CCPA compliance as a competitive advantage?
- How to de-risk your business from private litigation?

As you take your first steps for CCPA compliance, you need actionable advice. You may need advice to rethink your data strategy. This is the book for you.

Why this book

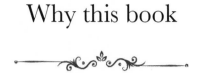

As a business, you need data. You need data about your markets, your customers, your potential customers, your partners, and more. You need a lot of it. You need to collect this data or buy it. The type of data, the amount of data you have, and how you use this data will determine the future of your business. If you think 'data is the new oil,' you already understand the value of data for your business.

CCPA is a big bump on the road to your data strategy. California legislature does not intend to destroy the tech economy built on data, and data-driven companies. So, why did the California legislature enact CCPA? It is because privacy had become a major concern for the California consumer, and timing was just right for the legislature to act. This book does not cover the history of privacy or the reasons behind the actions of the California legislature.

Apple, Google, Facebook, Microsoft, Amazon, and several large tech companies have made substantial investments in being data-driven companies. Microsoft announced that it will honor consumer rights under CCPA throughout the United States. New and upcoming privacy laws in other states on lines similar to CCPA are intended to encourage businesses to enforce their own privacy policies.

Large tech companies do not perceive CCPA as a threat to their data strategy. This is because the right to privacy is built-in into their privacy policies. These companies may need to implement a few programs to address specific requirements towards CCPA compliance. However, they are not concerned that CCPA is a major risk to their business. It does not change their business model.

CCPA takes effect on Jan 1, 2020. Several large companies have teams already working on CCPA compliance. Most mid-size and small businesses are unaware of the law. They need to engage their legal and IT teams to implement compliance.

So, this book helps you to find a specific path for your business. A path that ensures CCPA compliance. A path that assures your data strategy survives CCPA. A path that is fast and easy to implement. A path that is not expensive. A path that adds value to your customers, partners, and your investors.

In this book, I tried to be comprehensive. I am not an attorney. I have a deep background in security, technology, and business processes. Over the past 2 decades, I developed security products. I am a startup advisor, and I worked extensively with technology titans including Intel, Samsung, IBM, and many more. This book draws upon my expertise and experience to provide a detailed view on how to implement CCPA compliance without significant changes to your business model or processes. For example, this book does not advocate a rush to map your business process or data flows. I do urge you to take action. If you need more clarity, I recommend that you get help.

Who is the ideal reader of this book?

The ideal reader of this book is an executive, entrepreneur, or business person who thinks compliance is a necessary evil. This book is for that executive who explores opportunities to add value as part of CCPA compliance. This book is for the CMO, who is building a strong data-driven culture in light of new privacy laws. This book is for the CIO, who is trying to balance priorities and budgets. This book is for the new DPO (data protection officer), who is trying to establish an effective privacy program. This book is about helping those executives deliver CCPA compliance on a budget, and mitigate risks.

How to make the best use of this book?

As a privacy law, the CCPA is about transparency, control, and security. I suggest you read this book from the perspective of implementation, goals, costs, and schedule.

First, this book provides you a path. A path that is your own, and not another template checklist of things to do. While you read this book, make a note of those items that do not apply to your business. It will save you a lot of time and resources. For example, if your business does not sell data then it substantially reduces the scope of your implementation.

Second, this book gives you enough knowledge to ask the right questions. These questions will help you chart out the path for your business. Questions that prevent you from going down the wrong rabbit hole. Questions that you can ask your IT team. Questions that prevent expensive IT projects. Questions that you can ask your marketing and legal teams.

Third, this book gives you a number of ideas. Ideas to add value. Ideas to get more out of your investment. Ideas that help you leverage your investment. For example, I discuss a communication plan to engage your partners and b2b customers. This is an opportunity for your account team to have a face to face meetings and improve interaction and trust.

To make it easier for the reader, each chapter has "**Actions**" section at the end. These actions will make your implementation quicker and less expensive. And, these actions help you reduce your cyber liability insurance costs. I am confident that you will gain a good understanding of consumer rights to privacy, and achieve CCPA compliance in a short time.

Introduction

Let's get a bird's view of what is happening with Data Privacy and privacy regulations. Most companies are being forced to review their privacy policies and data strategies. This is either a result of CCPA (California Consumer Privacy Act) (Legislature A. 3., 2018), GDPR (EU, 2016) (General Data Protection Regulation), or a number of other potential privacy laws in motion. Several states in the US are actively considering laws similar to CCPA, and a number of countries are enacting their own version of GDPR.

**"I used to bury my bones.
Now I upload them to the cloud."**

Nearly all of the new regulatory activity is driven by three key themes, protect consumer privacy, provide transparency on data collection, and lastly, provide security as it is related to data theft prevention.

The result is, a few companies are getting proactive. Apple (Apple, 2019) is focused on differentiating themselves using privacy.

> *"Right now, there is more private information on your phone than in your home. Think about that. So many details about your life right in your pocket. This makes privacy more important now than ever.*
>
> *Your location, your messages, your heart rate after a run, these are private things. Personal things. And they should belong to you. Simple as that.*
>
> *We believe your privacy should never be something you have to question. It should be simple, straightforward, and understood."*
>
> *Apple Corporation, 'Privacy, that is iPhone' advertisement(s).*

Facebook published a new privacy-focused vision for social networking. Mark Zuckerberg (Zuckerberg, 2019) states:

> *"Outline our vision and principles around building a privacy-focused messaging and social networking platform. Public social networks will continue to be very important in people's lives. But now, with all the ways people also want to interact privately, there's also an opportunity to build a simpler platform that's focused on privacy first. This privacy-focused platform will be built around several principles: Private interactions,*

Encryption, Reducing Permanence, Safety, Interoperability, and Secure Data Storage.

I believe we should be working towards a world where people can speak privately and live freely, knowing that their information will only be seen by who they want to see it, and won't stick around forever. If we can help move the world in this direction, I will be proud of the difference we've made."

Microsoft announced that it will honor California's privacy rights throughout the United States. Julie Brill (Julie Brill, 2019), Microsoft's Chief Privacy Officer states:

"We are strong supporters of California's new law and the expansion of privacy protections in the United States that it represents. Our approach to privacy starts with the belief that privacy is a fundamental human right and includes our commitment to provide robust protection for every individual. This is why, in 2018, we were the first company to voluntarily extend the core data privacy rights included in the European Union's General Data Protection Regulation (GDPR) to customers around the world, not just to those in the EU who are covered by the regulation. Similarly, we will extend CCPA's core rights for people to control their data to all our customers in the U.S.

We continue to put these principles into practice every day through ongoing investments in tools that give people greater control over their personal information. More than 25 million people around the world – including over 10 million people in the U.S. – have used our privacy dashboard to understand and control their personal data. By being transparent about the data we collect and how we use it, and by providing solutions that empower businesses to safeguard personal data and comply with privacy laws, we can demonstrate our commitment in the absence of Congressional action."

Is there an urgency for your business? Yes. There is an urgency to address the issue of data privacy. This urgency is mainly driven by the need for CCPA compliance. CCPA is effective Jan 1, 2020. Most companies need to react to CCPA compliance. Apple and Facebook, despite their public stance, need to deliver CCPA compliance. In my discussions, several senior executives had objections regarding CCPA compliance. These objections imply that CCPA compliance does not apply to them.

- We are a b2b company. This is for consumers.
- We do not collect any data.
- We do not sell any data, we sell other things.
- The data is not useful to the consumers, so, they don't really want it.
- How about a Federal privacy policy?
- We don't store any of the data.
- The AG (Attorney General) has not finalized the regulations.
- California legislature is still considering several amendments.

- We have **GDPR** compliance.
- We have world-class security.
- We don't engage children.
- **GDPR** consumer requests are nearly zero.
- It is nearly impossible to address imprecise and expansive data requests.
- Cloud Service providers Salesforce, Microsoft, Google, have no privacy APIs to data.

I noticed during my discussions, that the underlying theme is to find a way out of committing a budget and resources for CCPA compliance. I shall detail whether CCPA applies to your business, and I shall discuss each of these objections throughout the book.

As of Nov 2019, there are scant statistics on the number of companies that started the implementation programs for CCPA compliance. But, estimates on budgets required for CCPA compliance are high. Over 70% of companies expect to spend more than $100,000 in IT and legal services. About 20% of companies are expected to spend over $1 Million. Most of the companies need help and expertise to understand the compliance requirements. These companies are likely to seek help in deploying the right technology, process, and legal help.

Compliance only approach is a Band-Aid. But it is an essential first step to avoid penalties. A security review is also necessary to avoid risks of private action resulting from data exfiltration (breach). I recommend that you revisit privacy as a strategy and competitive advantage in the future, and focus purely on compliance now. Get a team together fast.

The very first step is to identify if the CCPA applies to your business. It is imperative to determine if your business even needs to have CCPA compliance. If so, determine the level of urgency. This helps define a clear implementation goal for your team. Nearly 400,000 businesses are estimated to implement CCPA compliance. That is a very large number of businesses impacted by CCPA.

Next up is to get your team together. Time is short for the implementation. I shall discuss it in detail in Chapter 2. Once the team is together they have to be focused on the right goal.

Once you get your team together, it is time to figure out which parts of the CCPA are applicable to your business. I provided a simple table for you in Chapter 3. Your team needs to review the table and create a checklist of your requirements.

The logical step after this is to create a plan. I discussed that in Chapter 4. A plan needs to be executable with the right resources and a reasonable timeline. The date of implementation is Jan 1, 2020. However, you may get only a few activities completed by that time. It is important to plan, so you could finish the tasks required. A few tasks will take beyond Jan 1, 2020, to complete. It is imperative to ensure that the team continues the work beyond Jan 1, 2020, to finish these.

The team must, by now, have a resource and budget estimate for approval.

Now that you have a plan, it is time to get implementation help. I cover it in Chapter 5. A number of vendors provide tools and services for CCPA compliance. There is no magic bullet. No single tool or technology delivers end-to-end compliance. Most vendors are still coming up to speed on the regulations. But, you could stitch together tools that satisfy your compliance checklist.

Consumer privacy rights management is the key starting element for CCPA compliance. I discuss this in detail in Chapter 6. This applies to nearly all businesses. It also requires changes to notices and policies.

Data. It is about data discovery and lookup in Chapter 7. Your team may leverage work done as part of GDPR or other compliance requirements. This chapter details data mapping, 3rd party data inventory, contracts, and audit trail. I will specifically discuss the relationship between privacy rights management and access to personal data. If your data is spread across, I recommend Privacy APIs for data lookup. Most companies have a fairly good idea of their data assets. Rushing to do data flows and maps is not the smart answer. In this chapter, I detail out Privacy APIs and how to implement a long-term plan for continued compliance.

Security. This is a very big topic. In Chapter 8, I focus on the specific areas of security required for CCPA compliance. Privacy is not just about security. The CCPA has specific data security requirements.

Chapter 9 is a communications plan: your disclosures, your website, sending notices to your customers, partners, and other 3rd parties, establishing new internal policies, and communicating new privacy policy changes to your employees.

Chapter 10 is all about continued compliance - process, contracts, and amendments. The process to ensure continued compliance. This also includes external stakeholders, your service provider partners, and your suppliers. Training and governance also get some air in this chapter.

Let's get started.

Actions:

- Stop being in denial mode (See objections above).
- Accept CCPA compliance as a new normal.
- Be driven by CCPA compliance, and not a data strategy.
- Setup a budget, start with $50K or $100K.
- Get started with a small team of two people.

Things to Avoid:

- Do not over-think your privacy policy, there is no time for this.

Remember:

- January 1, 2020 is the effective date of CCPA.
- July 1, 2020 is start of enforcement action by California AG.

CHAPTER ONE

Do nothing

4 00,000 *businesses may be required to implement CCPA compliance. If your business is not one of them, then, it is best to know about that faster, and do nothing.*

The very first step is to identify if the CCPA applies to your business. It is imperative to determine if your business even needs to have CCPA compliance. If so, determine the level of urgency. This helps define a clear implementation goal for your team.

Let's explore the 'Do Nothing' approach. This is the best-case scenario.

You already bought this book. Let's assume you are concerned about this new law or, you are wondering whether you should be concerned. I started with the best-case scenario so you could paint a worry-free picture for your own business.

California Consumer Privacy Act (CCPA) applies to business entities that collect consumer personal information, and such entities that conduct business in the State of California. One of these conditions apply:

1. Earns annual gross revenues in excess of $25,000,000.

2. Buys and receives for commercial purposes; sells, or shares for commercial purposes, the personal information of 50,000 or more consumers, households (your tv, settop box, your wifi router, laptop, mobile phone, will each be included in the 50,000), or devices per year; or

3. Derives 50 percent or more of its annual revenues from selling consumers' personal information.

Let's quickly figure out if the CCPA applies to your business? That is quite easy. Check the table below. If your answer to the question is yes, write 1 in the yes column.

Conduct Business in California		
		Yes=1
Are you incorporated in California?	**1**	
Do you have locations in California?	**2**	
Do you derive revenue from California residents?	**3**	
	Total **(1+2+3)**	

Now, total up the yes column on the last row. Is your total 0? Then, 'Do Nothing' and return this book to get your money back. Is your total 1 or more? Then let's move on to the next table to determine applicability. If your answer to the question is yes, write 1 in the yes column.

CCPA Applicability		
		Yes=1
Are your estimated 2019 revenues > $25 Million?	**5**	
Does your website have over 961 California visitors in the last 7 days?	**6**	
Do you have over 50,000 contacts in your CRM/ other systems?	**7**	
	Total **(5+6+7)**	

Now, total up the yes column on the last row. Is your total 0? If you do not sell personal information, then 'Do Nothing,' return this book and get your money back. Most businesses do not sell the personal information they collect. This table above applies to most businesses. If you are a data service provider or sell personal information, then the next table applies to your business to determine applicability. If your answer to the question is yes, write 1 in the yes column.

Data as a service		
		Yes=1
Are you a free mobile/web app with 50,000+ users?	9	
Are you a data broker? Do you buy and sell personal data?	10	
Are you a service provider who (in)directly collects personal data?	11	
	Total (9+10+11)	

Check the total in 9+10+11 row. This may look like a simple exercise, but this will help you get your team to focus on the right goals. You will do more about the team and goals in the next chapter. Now, does CCPA does apply to you? Then let's explore how not to spend your well-earned profits on yet another regulation.

Some b2b businesses I talked to, believe that CCPA does not apply to them. When you replace the word consumer with California residents, you will notice how it applies to b2b businesses.

The question to answer now is, can you risk the 'Do Nothing' approach? For this, you need to explore the risk. The risk of non-compliance to CCPA is penalties and potential private action. Let's remember these two dates.

The effective date of the CCPA	January 1, 2020
Start date of CCPA enforcement by the AG	July 1, 2020 (est.)

You may not expect any penalties from California Attorney General until July 1, 2020. However, California AG may levy penalties for all violations starting January 1, 2020. Let's explore the cost of penalties, before we explore the cost of private action.

Enforcement risk

I am not an attorney, so I shall refrain from citing sections and titles in the law. Let's assume you did nothing, i.e., do not have an intake form, or change your privacy policy, or any other actions. Let me explain in simple terms, when and how penalties could be levied on your business.

Step 1: Consumer John Doe visits, calls your business or sends you an email.

Step 2: You do not respond for 30 days or more.

Step 3: John Doe then sends you a notice of action email and reports to the California AG.

Step 4: After July 1, 2020, California AG sends you a notice of non-compliance.

Step 5: You do not resolve the issue in 30 days, then you may get an enforcement penalty of $2,500 - $7,500.

Let's take an example to illustrate the size of penalties. Cambridge Analytica scandal was a key motivation for CCPA. If this scandal were to happen in 2020 or later, let's estimate the potential penalty on Facebook. Some estimates indicate 24.6 million California users were impacted. If California AG finds Facebook in violation, a penalty between $61.5 Billion and $184.5 Billion could be imposed on Facebook. This variance is based on if the violation was unintentional or intentional. Facebook settled this for $5 Billion with the FTC (Settlement F. F.).

In your 'Do Nothing' approach, if you estimate to receive no more than 10 penalties per year, then your risk is between $25,000 and $75,000. As you get more enforcement action, it may be considered an intentional violation and likely to draw $7,500 per enforcement action.

Private action risk

The 'Do Nothing' approach should also consider private action. This is a bit trickier.

Your business implemented cyber-security. You believe it is sufficient to prevent a data breach. However, a data exfiltration (breach) occurred. This includes records of 1000 California residents. My interpretation is simple. For private action, each record must have two or more pieces of personally identifiable information for the data breach to amount to a class action. For example, name and street address, or name and social security number, etc.

Step 1: One of the 1000 affected California residents initiates private action

Step 2: Your business has 30 days to cure (you cannot redact a data breach, so no cure)

Step 3: Plaintiff attorney aggregates it into a class

Step 4: Your business has no cure for another 30 days

Step 5: The class seeks damages of $750,000

Let's take an example to illustrate the size of penalties. The cost of Equifax data breach is estimated at $1.4 Billion. Let's estimate the potential plaintiff class action on Equifax in 2020 or later. Some estimates indicate 15 million California users were impacted. The plaintiff class action damages can be between $1.5 Billion and

$11.25 Billion. Equifax settled this for $700 Million with the FTC (Settlement F.), much of this being in services rendered.

In your 'Do Nothing' approach, if you estimate 1 data breach per year of 10,000 records, then your risk is between $1 Million and $7.5 Million per year. Just evaluate your risk and Do Something.

Actions:
- Resolve to – Do Something.
- Get your team to define the priorities.

Things to Avoid:
- Do not overdo the risk assessment, just get your team started.

Remember:
- Your first enforcement action may be after July 2, 2020.
- Your first private action could be after Jan 2, 2020.

CHAPTER TWO

Start something

G etting started implies you need a plan. Let's first identify what you already have. You have a team selected to lead through this process. You gave the team a small budget. They have clear goals. The goals are:

1. Avoid enforcement action.

2. Avoid private action.

3. Be on budget.

4. As soon as Jan 1, 2020, and no later than June 30, 2020.

My experience with project management teams is simple. As a sponsoring executive, you can control only one out of three things - resources, scope, or schedule. You need to decide which is more important for you. Let's assume you want control over resources and budget. You must relinquish control over the scope and schedule to the project lead.

You need to give your project team specific guidance and limits on the budget and human resources. This does not imply that full compliance is a dream. It does imply that the project lead could prioritize tasks that best avoid enforcement and private action. And, there is a slight schedule flexibility, so long as your business shows intent to address full compliance.

Let's identify the type of internal resources that your project team needs. It is necessary to bridge the gap between business needs, consumer expectations, and compliance. Your customers have expectations on privacy. Your goal is to avoid enforcement action and private action. Your CMOs' goal is to meet/exceed consumer expectations and expand the trust in your brand. Your CIOs' goal is to support and secure the data.

Your CCPA compliance team needs representatives from legal, IT, and marketing. For some specific tasks, you may need extended support from procurement and sales teams.

Your project team will need external help. This external help may be in the form of tools, expertise, or both. Let's first talk about expertise. Law firms and consulting firms provide expertise. Insurance brokers and firms may have cyber policy changes for CCPA. This book does not cover cyber insurance vendors. Tool vendors also provide consulting and expertise, along with their technology or tools. Often, they provide a CCPA compliance framework similar to GDPR. You will also get a few sales pitches from vendors that include manual privacy request processing. Certified privacy professionals or privacy attorneys process individual privacy requests for you on a time and material basis. In my view, this service gets expensive, fast. Often the CCPA experts are too busy with many clients. I agree that there will be certain types of privacy requests that need closer scrutiny by a legal or privacy expert.

Let's discuss the vendor's tools that you need for CCPA compliance. I provided a good reference to the vendor's tool in the appendix. Technology tools take the form of:

- Privacy request intake
- Data lookup (associated with the intake)
- Data security (associated with private action)

I will discuss tools and external help in more detail in Chapter 5. The intent of providing a brief detail in this chapter is to provide a rough estimate of budget and resources.

The overall projected economic estimate of the initial compliance costs is $16 Billion (California A.). CNBC reports that CCPA could cost companies a total of $55 Billion (CNBC, Lauren Feiner, 2019) to get to compliance. These estimates assume that about 75 percent of businesses in California may need to comply with CCPA. What is the cost estimate for your business? A majority of small and mid-size businesses are expected to spend a little over $100K. A few businesses expect to spend over a million.

Often, GDPR is used as a yardstick for CCPA compliance. However, I believe that the CCPA has more clear regulations. The following table provides a guideline for budgeting, in addition to the internal resources responsible for achieving CCPA compliance.

Item	Budget Estimate (Businesses with Revenue of)	
	Less than $100 Million	Over $100 Million
Process related		
Legal	$ 25K - $ 50K	$ 500K - $ 1 Million
Data assessment, mapping, & discovery	$ 25K - $ 50K	$ 250K - $ 500K
Ongoing request processing (yearly)	$ 50K - $ 75K	$ 75K - $ 150K
SANS(CIS) Top 20 security assessment	$ 25K - $ 150K	$ 100K - $ 250K
Tools		
Privacy request intake software (yearly)	$ 5K - $ 15K	$ 25K - $ 100K
Data lookup (One-time cost)	$ 15K - $ 25K	$ 15K - $ 25K
Data security (per user per year)	$ 100	$ 100

The budget estimates for data lookup varies, depending on the number of IT systems your business uses. To lookup personal information, several IT systems may need to be connected. This is both an expensive and time-consuming task. Using your internal teams will substantially reduce this cost. The cost of securing data is fairly deterministic and is about $100 - $150 per user per year. Depending on the type of data security you deploy, you may not need to spend on data mapping. Based on the above table, your team will have the ability to create a fair estimate for your initial compliance costs. The team must also create a budget for ongoing compliance costs. I also recommend budgeting for cyber liability insurance (not added in the budgetary estimates above).

The above budgetary estimates are for large California businesses. This estimate could be $100K - $250K for small and mid-size businesses. However, service providers, data brokers, and software companies need to make special and separate assessments. The effort required for these businesses is a bit more substantial. Budgetary estimates for small and mid-size service providers could be upwards of $250K.

Actions:

- Assemble the internal team.
- Talk to 2-3 external law firms and vendors.
- Create an initial budget estimate.

Things to Avoid:

- Over budgeting for security assessment.

Remember:

- Identify internal team to do the data lookup over time.
- Do training to reduce the cost of request processing.

CHAPTER THREE

The regulations

In this chapter, you shall identify the regulations that apply to your business, and prioritize them for implementation. The CCPA regulations (California A. G.) and subsequent business requirements can be broadly classified into these categories:

- Notices & policy changes
- Response to privacy requests
- Data lookup and access
- Data security
- Data as a service business

Most businesses do not sell the personal information they collect. This eliminates a number of requirements listed below. Use this table below to establish the scope of your CCPA compliance.

	Required (Y/N)	Priority (1,2,3)
Notices & Changes		
Notice of personal information collection – pop-up		
Notice of collected personal information – categories		
Notice of collected personal information – purpose(s)		
Notice of collected personal information - sources		
Notice of personal information collection – the link		
Notice of indirect personal information collection		
Right to opt-out of sale – notice		
Financial incentive – notice		
Verification process – notice		
Privacy policy – combined notice		
Response to privacy requests		
Privacy request intake management (tool)		
Privacy requests – definitions		
Privacy requests – methods		

Privacy requests indirect consumers – methods		
Privacy requests – email templates for communication		
Privacy requests – acknowledgment		
Privacy requests – response		
Response – right to know categories		
Response – right to know purposes		
Response – right to know sources		
Response – right to know categories of 3rd parties		
Response – right to access personal information		
Response – right to access information sold to 3rd parties		
Response – right to delete personal information		
Response – 'Do Not Sell My Personal Information'		
Response – secure transmission		
Response – Password-protected accounts		
Privacy requests – household information		
Request verification process		
Email verification		
One time password (2FA verification)		

Consumers with password-protected accounts		
Partners / Suppliers		
Provide a reference to the privacy page		
Amend agreement – Covenant to comply with CCPA		
Request intake if data is bought from 3rd party		
Vendor risk assessment		
Customers		
B2B - amend agreements to include CCPA compliance		
Provide privacy page update notification		
Data lookup		
Inventory of all cloud and internal apps		
Privacy APIs to relevant apps upon request intake		
Data security		
Data breach prevention (DLP)		
Data encryption		
Data anonymization		
Training & audit		
Request processors – training		
Audit trail &information		

You may have a number of IT systems, leverage them for several of the above requirements. Prioritization helps further define the scope and helps in planning. Let's discuss these in detail.

Notices & policy changes

Notice of personal information collection – pop-up: If you collect personal information, you must inform consumers that you collect personal information. On your website, you need to place a clear notice in simple English. I recommend this footer pop-up notice.

> "We collect your personal information. Click here for more (link to your privacy page)."

If you can track returning consumers on your website, then you may not have to display this notice for returning consumers. Do you publish your website in multiple languages? You need to have the notice in all the languages you support.

Notice of personal information collection – categories: Do you collect personal information? Then, you need to list the categories of personal information you collect. Get your list together. Publish this list on your website. You disclose a generic list of all categories on your website. In addition, you need to be able to provide, when requested by the consumer, a specific list of categories to each consumer that submits a privacy request. Here is a sample list of categories that you could use:

Internet or network activities
Device-specific information
Commercial information (ex: orders, history, credit card data, etc.)
Identifying information (ex: email, phone, etc.)
Health information
Biometric information
Fitness information
Professional or employment-related information
Educational information
Geolocation information
Audio/Video information
Automotive information
Information users share
Information to process privacy requests

Notice of personal information collection – purpose(s): You collect personal information. Then, you need to list the purpose of the personal information you collect. Get your list together for each category. Publish this list on your website. You need to disclose a generic list of all purposes under each category on your website. In addition, you need to be able to provide a specific list of purposes under specific categories to each consumer that submits a privacy request for categories of information collected. Here is a sample list of purposes that you could use:

To Enforce Policies, Terms, and Conditions
To Track and Monitor Website Usage
To Analyze Website Visitor Behavior
To Improve Website Performance
To Improve Visitor Engagement
To Service Customers
To Provide Sales and Support
To Answer Questions or Address Requests
To Evaluate Suitable Candidates for Jobs
To Create User Accounts
To Communicate Marketing and Sales Promotions
To Communicate Company Policy Information
To Fill and Manage Sales Orders and Support Requests
To Write Testimonials
To Deliver Advertisements
To Get Customer Feedback
To Share Data With Data Brokers
To Aid in Research
To Aid in Behavioral Analysis
To Process Privacy Requests

Notice of personal information collection – source(s): You need to list the sources of personal information you collect. Collect your list and publish it on your website. You need to disclose a generic list of all sources on your website. In addition, you need to be able to provide a specific list of sources to each consumer that submits a privacy request. Here is a sample list of sources that you could use:

Laptops and Desktops
Websites
Desktop Apps
Web Apps
Mobile Apps
Shopping Carts
Phone Calls
Fitness Devices
Mobile Devices
Video Streaming Devices
Medical Devices
Smart Speakers
Smart Toys
Security Cameras
Wi-Fi Routers
Automotive Sensors
Smart Sensors & Scanners
Tablets
Data Services
3rd Party Data Brokers
Social Media Platforms
Advertising Platforms

Notice of personal information collection – the link: In one of the requirements above, I detailed a link in a footer popup on your website. This link needs to display several sections in plain English or other languages you publish on your website. These sections are:

- List of categories
- List of reasons per category
- List of sources
- Link to the privacy policy
- Link to the privacy request form
  - A specific for 'Do Not Sell My Info' button
- Or, link to a privacy policy, and provide all these sections in the privacy policy

Notice of indirect personal information collection: If you are not in the business of selling or licensing personal information, then this CCPA regulation is not meant for you, you can mark this requirement as not required.

If your business sells/shares/licenses personal information, then you need to prioritize this requirement. Contact the source(s) of your data. Your sources need to attest that they conform to the CCPA notices and disclosures. However, if you store data with your service providers, check the sections that address the CCPA regulations for service providers.

Right to opt-out of sale – notice: Do you sell or have plans to sell personal information collected? If the answer is no, then state this clearly in your privacy policy. And you may mark your scope document accordingly. And, if the answer is yes, then state it clearly in your privacy policy.

"We sell (or plan to sell) some or all of the personal information we collect. To opt-out of this, please click the button below."

> **Do Not Sell My Personal Information**

This button is additionally mandated by the CCPA regulations. And, you must publish this in all the languages you use on your website. You may add a logo to the above button or link.

Financial incentive – notice: A few businesses offer a free service for collecting and selling personal information. Similar to Facebook, some of these businesses may not sell personal information and potentially provide a platform for advertising and revenue generation. Several similar revenue generation models are prevalent. The CCPA regulations clarify how a business can provide a financial incentive for collection and/or sale. You need to make this clear in your privacy notice. Any such privacy notice must include a clear statement that consumers can withdraw anytime, and must include a process for consumers to change their choice. A consumer may withdraw using the 'Do Not Sell My Personal Information' button or link. You may additionally want to provide a way to opt-in to the sale of personal information. In the above example of Facebook like platform, it is clear such platforms do not sell personal information. The exception being sharing the information with 3rd party partners such as Cambridge Analytica using APIs and partner programs. You may want to re-evaluate your partner programs for sharing personal information and potentially consider a financial incentive in such partner program participation.

Verification process – notice: Verification process is a means to verify the consumer who submits a privacy request. A verification process is required to address the privacy requests from consumers. For CCPA compliance, you need to state the verification process and methods used clearly. For example, if your verification process requires an email verification, you need to state what the process is, and why you need email verification. More on verification is detailed in chapter 5.

Privacy policy – combined notice: You are required to have a privacy policy on your website. It is likely that you have a privacy policy on your website today. For CCPA compliance, you need to have a privacy policy in plain English. I recommend the creation of two versions of the privacy policy.

- Version 1 is a plain English version
- Version 2 is what you have today modified for CCPA compliance, a legal version

If your website is published in multiple languages, your privacy policy needs to support this. In addition, I recommend publishing audio of the plain English version, and providing a download file for both versions.

Response to privacy requests

Privacy request intake management: Nearly all businesses need this tool. A privacy request intake tool helps your business to increase productivity. As a part of GDPR, several businesses provide a toll-free number, or an email address for privacy requests. Expensive privacy professionals representing these businesses, listen to voicemail, or pour through emails to decode the privacy requests. A web form for privacy intake is less expensive, more effective, and substantially reduces errors. I recommend a privacy request intake (aka DSAR) web software app from a 3rd party vendor. A detailed discussion of such vendors is in Chapter 5.

Privacy requests – definitions: The CCPA grants the right to privacy to a consumer (aka California resident). A privacy request is a way to exercise this right to privacy. A consumer has the right to several types of privacy requests. These specific requests are:

- Right to know categories of information collected
- Right to know the purpose(s) of information collection for each category

- Right to know the source(s) of information collection for each category
- Right to know categories of 3rd parties the information is sold/disclosed for each category
- Right to access information
- Right to access information sold/disclosed to 3rd party
- Right to delete personal information
- Do Not Sell My Personal Information

Privacy requests – methods: A privacy request is a way for a consumer to submit a privacy request of one of the types listed above. A web form is a first and recommended choice for privacy requests, submitted by the consumer. It is an easy method to provide for all types of privacy requests. This reduces submission errors, and it simplifies requester verification.

A second method is also required for CCPA compliance. I recommend a 1-800 or other toll-free numbers. IVR (interactive voice response) and a combination of bots could be used to fully automate requests using a toll-free number. IVR substantially reduces errors in submission. Automation also helps to improve requester verification. Your business may use other methods such as submission via email (ex: privacy-requests@companydomain. com), a downloadable form to submit through the mail (US Postal Service or other), or a form available at your retail service centers or shopping location(s).

For retail shops or businesses that have a consumer-facing location, you are required to provide disclosures and privacy request intake methods on-site. For example, if you are a car dealer or a coffee shop, and the

CCPA applies to you, then you need to prominently display a privacy notice and provide a way for consumers to exercise their right to privacy at all your locations.

For online only businesses, a second method is not required. Providing a web form for privacy request submission is sufficient.

Privacy requests indirect consumers – methods: If you are a service provider, you must have at least one method for the indirect consumer to submit privacy requests. A web form is the recommended method, and this is consistent with direct consumer's request.

Privacy requests – email templates for communication: Your business must have a standard way to communicate with the requesting consumer. This will help create a repeatable process and reduces the cost of request processing. Use email templates listed below. These are starting email template examples, to kick off your request processing.

Privacy requests – acknowledgment: The CCPA regulations require that you acknowledge the receipt of the privacy request promptly within 10 days. As part of this receipt, you may include an email verification link, any additional verification steps or process, timeline to expect a response, and response to multiple requests, if any.

Type of notification email	When used	#
Email verification notification	Upon receipt of privacy request	One
Privacy request acknowledgment	Send once verification is done depending on settings	One
Privacy request is assigned to you	Send to the request processor once assigned	One
Privacy request legal review completed/rejected	Send to the request processor upon this status	One
Privacy request processing extension	Sent to the requestor by the request processor	One
Purpose of collecting personal information	Sent to the requestor by request processor	Many
Categories of personal data collected	Sent to the requestor by request processor	Many
Sources of personal data collected	Sent to the requestor by request processor	Many
Personal data access request	Sent to the requestor by request processor(Attach file)	Many
Request access to data sold/shared	Sent to the requestor by request processor(Attach file)	Many
Request - Do Not Sell My Personal Info	Sent to the requestor by request processor	Many
Request – Delete My personal info	Sent to the requestor by request processor	Many
Privacy request is rejected	Sent to the requestor by request processor	Many

Privacy requests – response timeline: California AG's CCPA regulations require a response in 45 days from the date of the privacy request submittal. This is different from an earlier interpretation of 45 days from the date of verification of the request. You may respond with an extension of an additional 45 days. An extension response to the privacy requests must include a reason for the extension. Get help from your legal team to interpret. For example, what happens if the verification is incomplete? If the verification of the consumer request is not complete, you have two choices;

a) deny the request indicating the incomplete verification as the reason for denial, or

b) send an extension of another 45 days to complete, with a request of incomplete verification as the reason for an extension.

Response – right to know categories: The right to know requests are a bit tricky. However, the CCPA regulations provide clarification on how the responses need to be addressed. The regulations imply that data categories are the basis for structuring the data collection. I recommend separating the right to know by consumer type, as I detail in this section.

The response to a request for the right to know the categories shall be the categories for the specific consumer type. Treat these as individual privacy requests to comply with the CCPA. This may sound a bit of a stretch, but I recommend that you document categories by the type of consumer. This practice will ensure rapid response to this type of privacy request. If the privacy request cannot be verified, I recommend a response with general information for the right to know requests.

Response – right to know purposes: This is similar to the above discussion on the right to know categories. As a business practice, it is best to collect purposes under each category. I also recommend separating the purposes by consumer (requester) type. This will ensure the individualized response to each consumer.

Response – right to know sources: This is also similar to the right to know purposes. Follow the same practices, so individualized responses can be communicated to the consumer.

Response – right to know categories of 3rd parties: Check on the response to a right to know categories above. If your business does not sell/disclose personal information to other 3rd parties, you still have to respond, indicating that you do not sell / disclose personal information to 3rd parties. Be aware of sending stock responses. Let's consider this gotcha example.

Step 1, a consumer asks for a right to know categories of 3rd parties.

Step 2, (s)he gets a response.

Step 3, (s)he submits an opt-out of sale request.

Step 4, you respond.

Step 5, (s)he then asks again for the right to know categories of 3rd parties.

Step 6, you send the same stock response; this may imply that the opt-out has been unsuccessful. This may imply a violation of the CCPA regulations.

Response – right to access personal information: The CCPA regulations provide general guidance about the disclosure of types of information about the consumer. It does not provide any guidance on the extent of personal information. It states all personal information. This area of the regulation intentionally broad. I recommend to the extent applicable to provide all the information. For example, a salesperson stores personal notes about a key customer in the CRM system; upon request, does your privacy request response include these personal, often embarrassing notes? This customer has the right to know. My interpretation is that these personal notes are considered personal information, and must be included as response to the consumer.

The CCPA compliance requires disclosure of all information, metadata, and any related data. One area that is clear, is what not to include. As part of the response, you are not to disclose (include in the response) any information that is:

- Personally identifiable data such as:
  - Social security number
  - Driver license number

- Government-issued identifications
- Financial account numbers (ex: credit card numbers)
- Health care numbers or medical ids
- Account passwords or numbers
- Account security questions or answers
  - Information that conflicts with other federal or state law(s)
    - State clearly which law and type of information withheld
  - Creates a risk to the security of (I infer this as either a personal security risk or cyber risk)
    - The information disclosed
    - Consumer's account
    - Your business systems
    - Your network

A discussion on verification is important here. Responses to the wrong consumer with data may imply data exfiltration (breach) and may result in a private action. So, you need to be diligent with your verification process. If any step of the verification process fails, you may respond with a rejection of the request. You may consider OTP (one-time-password) verification or verification using 2FA (two-factor authentication).

My opinion is that the CCPA regulations cannot be considered as a rule in this situation. In responding to the right to access information, I recommend caution. Confirmation of the request is important prior to sending the data and response. This is specifically the case for non-account (i.e. no consumer portal) based requests. Two-step verification could mean email verification, followed by a phone call. For password-protected accounts, login into the account, followed by request to confirm the privacy request in form of email, phone call or re-entering different credentials.

Response – right to access information sold to 3rd parties: Similar to the above right to access information, I recommend adding this type of privacy request to your intake form. This addresses a core premise of information collection and right to privacy. However, if your schedule does not permit this, you may prioritize this as 2 or 3.

If your business is involved in the sale/disclosure of data to 3rd parties, then the consumer would like to know the information sold/disclosed to 3rd parties. This is likely to address the specific information requests included in the CCPA regulations. Your attorney may provide a better interpretation of your business.

The response to this request is similar to the response to the right to access the information request discussed above. I recommend diligence in verification, prior to sending a response to non-account based requests.

Response – right to delete personal information: The regulations are clear, you must verify this request. No verification can default to denial of the request. Review the previous section for details on verification.

I recommend that you provide an all or nothing choice for deletion. The CCPA regulations give your business the ability to retain certain categories of data. You could do this by providing the consumer with an option to delete specific categories of personal information. This could be taxing on your business systems and process. This will likely increase the cost of your compliance.

CCPA regulations require you to process a response with;

a) permanently and completely erasing the personal information on its existing systems with the exception of archived or back-up systems

b) de-identifying the personal information

c) aggregating the personal information

d) retain a copy of the data only as part of an audit to this privacy request (or other states of federal laws), and

e) include the way in which the data is deleted.

You may reject the deletion of all data or specific data, and must include all of the information in your response to the request. A response with rejections or denials must include

a) reason for not deleting the specific data under regulation or statutory exception

b) must confirm that all other data is deleted, and

c) cannot use the data outside of the regulatory exception.

Response - 'Do Not Sell My Personal Information': This is one of the most discussed privacy right. This privacy request receives a special mention in the CCPA regulations. For CCPA compliance of this type of privacy request, your business must:

1. Provide a web form with the words 'Do Not Sell My Personal Information' or 'Do Not Sell My Info.' The intent is to remove ambiguity and provide consistency to consumers.

2. Provide a second method. I recommend an automated 1-800-Service, which I discussed earlier in this chapter.

You have 15 days to comply with this request. Verification of the consumer is not mandated for this type of privacy request. You must notify the consumer that the request is processed within 15 days.

If you sold/disclosed this consumer's data to a 3rd party, you must notify all the affected 3rd parties. You have 90 days to complete the notification. This implies that you need to modify your agreements with 3rd parties to ensure their CCPA compliance. Finally, you must notify the consumer that all 3rd parties have been notified of their opt-out request.

If you believe you received a fraudulent request, then you may not comply. But you must document why you perceive that you received a fraudulent request. The regulations are unclear on identifying fraudulent requests. There are no established practices. It is best to apply caution in establishing fraud.

Response – secure transmission: Your business must take reasonable security precautions while responding to the requests. This could be one of several items:

a) If the response is by email, ensure that the email is verified

b) If the response is in the form of a letter, ensure that the address is verified

c) If the response using a portal:

    a. Ensure that the portal using appropriate security (HTTPS, firewall, etc.)

    b. Ensure that the account to access the portal is authenticated

Response – password-protected accounts: If your business maintains user accounts and the requester is an account holder, then these privacy request-response mechanisms apply:

- Privacy requests for account holders can be inside a secure portal
- Privacy request submittals shall not require account access
- You may ask for additional verification
  - You may not restrict access to personal information within the portal
  - A way to download the information should be provided

Response – household information requests: Does your business process household information? For example, a cable operator or internet access provider, is likely to have household information. Household information is related to one or more consumers that are part of the household. Any household-related privacy request should be processed similar to an individual consumer privacy request. However, your business has the option to verify each member (consumer) of the household.

Verification process: In addition to the discussion on the verification process earlier, there are other requirements of verification address in the regulations. Let's summarize and add to that discussion.

All requests, except opt-out requests, must be verified. Opt-out requests must be processed without verification, unless you consider them fraudulent. This is indeed a high bar for opt-out requests. You may have to implement or deploy security measures to detect fraud, which implies expense and schedule issues. In my opinion, you may consider fraud detection as priority 3.

For the purposes of verification, you may ask for name, email address, phone number, and postal address. However, I recommend that you do not require submission of 2 or more pieces of information that is personally identifiable, at the time of privacy request submission. For example, do not ask (mandate) for a combination of name and social security number, or driver license number or ID card, or account number (credit card, etc.), or medical id, or health id. You may use a 3rd party verification service such as a KYC (know your customer) service to address these. A word of caution about KYC, most KYC services requires atleast 3 forms of personally identifiable information.

Data lookup and access

Data discovery and associated data lookup is the big elephant in the room. Scoping the data lookup and data deletion task is a difficult exercise. A report published by Cloud Security Alliance indicates businesses with less than 1000 employees run an average of 22 applications, and businesses with over 50,000 employees run an average of 788 applications. Some of these are custom applications, and some are 3rd party cloud-based applications. I discuss data lookup and privacy APIs in detail in chapter 7. At this stage, I recommend that your data lookup task should have a lower priority. The inventory of all cloud and internal apps should have a priority 1 or 2, but the automating data lookup using privacy APIs upon request intake should have a priority of 3. This is an involved task, and even if you received a privacy request for data access, you have additional 60 days to comply. And during the first 60 days you could provide lookup for the most obvious data for the consumer.

While I discussed this topic in detail in chapter 7, I feel it is important to differentiate these closely related terms and tools - data mapping, data discovery, and data lookup or access. While all these tools are useful, each of them serves a different purpose. Data mapping tools find out where your data is. Data discovery tools use the data map to classify the type of data and type of sensitivity. Data lookup and access tools read, modify, or delete the data. A few data discovery tools may provide a way to address data lookup. Check with the vendors that you are likely to evaluate.

Data security

"I'm applying for the Information Security position. Here is a copy of my resumé, encoded, encrypted and shredded."

Data security is a small but critical part of the CCPA privacy regulation. Specifically, there are two areas of data security consideration. The first is implementing 'reasonable security procedures' to address the exfiltration (breach) of unencrypted and non-redacted personal information. The second is the anonymization of data upon request for data deletion from a consumer. I shall discuss these in more detail in chapter 7. For the purpose of proper scoping your CCPA compliance plan, I feel that a quick brief is necessary on 'reasonable security procedures.'

SANS, a security organization had in previous years recommended 20 controls. It is now interpreted as the Center for Internet Security's (CIS) critical security controls. Implementing these controls may not avoid data exfiltration (breach) or plaintiff class-actions. However, not implementing these may be interpreted as a lack of reasonable security. Here is the list that you may reference at the CIS website (CISecurity). I discuss CSC 13 – data protection in more detail in chapter 8.

CSC 1: Inventory of Authorized and Unauthorized Devices
CSC 2: Inventory of Authorized and Unauthorized Software
CSC 3: Secure Configurations for Hardware and Software on Mobile Devices, Laptops, Workstations, and Servers
CSC 4: Continuous Vulnerability Assessment and Remediation
CSC 5: Controlled Use of Administrative Privileges
CSC 6: Maintenance, Monitoring, and Analysis of Audit Logs
CSC 7: Email and Web Browser Protections
CSC 8: Malware Defenses
CSC 9: Limitation and Control of Network Ports, Protocols and Services
CSC 10: Data Recovery Capability

CSC 11: Secure Configurations for Network Devices, such as Firewalls, Routers, and Switches
CSC 12: Boundary Defense
CSC 13: Data Protection
CSC 14: Controlled Access Based on the Need to Know
CSC 15: Wireless Access Control
CSC 16: Account Monitoring and Control
CSC 17: Security Skills Assessment and Appropriate Training to Fill Gaps
CSC 18: Application Software Security
CSC 19: Incident Response and Management
CSC 20: Penetration Tests and Red Team Exercises

Data as a service business

Service provider – privacy requests: Are you a service provider? If you are a SaaS business or a digital marketing business, then you must provide consumers with methods to submit privacy requests. For service providers' own businesses, it is likely that you collect personal information of your own customers and partners. Or collect personal information of potential customers and partners. CCPA compliance is necessary for such a service provider. (IAPP)

Next up, you collect information on behalf of your customers. For example, Google Analytics, CRM systems, digital marketing agencies, and many others collect personal information on behalf of their customers. In these situations, you are likely to receive privacy requests. Such requests must have a response. If the response is a denial, you must clearly state the reason for denial. For example, the denial could be that you have no access or right to access to the personal information collected on behalf of your customers.

As a service provider, you are required to collect, store, update, and present a link to privacy policy terms, or contact information of each of your customers (your tenants). If a consumer submits a privacy request, you are required to provide the privacy policy contact information for your customer (your tenant) to which the request belongs.

This is a bit tricky. You may collect privacy request contact information from each of your customers. You may be required to either provide a webpage link to all of that information. Often as a service provider, you do not have access to the personal information collected by each of your customers (tenants). This implies that you cannot respond to the privacy request submitted. Additionally, you may not infer the referencing customer (tenant) the privacy request is meant for. As a result, you may have to provide a link that lists all your customers' (tenants) privacy request contact information or privacy page links. I recommend providing a list of privacy page links to all customers' privacy terms.

If the consumer submitting the privacy request is an account holder, the situation will be different. In this situation, I recommend that you deploy and support privacy APIs that each of your customers (tenants) could use. This is similar to providing a CCPA compliance module as part of your service.

Service providers, specifically software companies, need to add a new privacy data lookup service to their offering. It is best to provide this, using privacy APIs. Privacy APIs needed for CCPA compliance include:

1. Look up data by consumer email, consumer phone number, or both

2. Look up data sold by consumer email, consumer phone number, or both

3. Execute opt-out of sale by consumer email, consumer phone number; or both

4. Execute opt into sale by consumer email, consumer phone number; or both

5. Execute delete data of consumer by consumer email, consumer phone number, or both

Of course, the API access must have a secure access mechanism with API secret and keys. If your business already provides API access, these APIs are an extension of your existing API service and infrastructure.

Actions:

- Get the team to identify and prioritize requirements.
- Get external help, unless you already have a CCPA expertise on your team.

Things to Avoid:

- Data lookup scoping is a daunting task, scope it lower and come back later.
- Re-interpreting data security scoping if you already have a CISO.

Remember:

- If you do not sell personal information your scope should be small.
- Finish this step in a few days, at most a week.

CHAPTER FOUR

The plan

Let's review what you have completed so far. The main goals of CCPA compliance are;

a. avoid enforcement action,

b. avoid private action to the extent possible,

c. be on budget, and

d. maintain a schedule.

You have a base budget, and in the previous chapter, I discussed scope and prioritization. The next logical step is to create a plan. This plan needs to be easy to execute and have a reasonable timeline. Let's remember these dates.

Effective data of the CCPA	January 1, 2020
Start date of CCPA enforcement by the AG	July 1, 2020 (estimated)
Enforcement action likely begin date	July 2, 2020
Relief date to respond to enforcement action	Aug 2, 2020

Now, it is time to start creating a project plan. Below is a list of major tasks to be performed for CCPA compliance. Each task needs to have an owner for taking the accountability to complete the task.

Select owners from the core team to get CCPA ready. Each owner would then decide the start and end date of each task. This is project management 101.

Kickoff
Complete CCPA Applicability Assessment
Evaluate CCPA consulting vendors
Evaluate Privacy Request Intake Software Vendors
Collect Data Collection Categories
Collect Data Collection Purpose by Category
Collect Data Collection Sources
Collect 3rd party categories (that you sell to)
Create a list of partners and customers
Applications that store personal information (inventory)
Determine scope of privacy APIs for service providers
Create generic privacy amendments
Website disclosures and changes
Execute communication plan
Top 20 Security controls assessment
Assess data security tools vendors & deploy
Assess data lookup tools and vendors & deploy
Assess CCPA training& get training for the team
Audit all activities

I added a detailed list of tasks and sub-tasks in the appendix for reference. Once you have the list of tasks and sub-tasks, it is easier for each owner to identify and leverage resources within the organization. It is likely that some, if not many, of these tasks are completed for other projects or initiatives. For example, getting a list of customers, partners, and their contact information should be readily available. Another example would be an inventory of cloud and internal apps. Your IT team should have a list of these assets readily available.

The next step is to assign ownership. I recommend that ownership for each of the main tasks stays with the core team. Each owner may have multiple sub-tasks assigned and owned by external team members. Alternately, the project team could hire a CCPA expert to drive these tasks to completion on-time and on-budget.

Service providers or software companies should add an additional key task to this list. That is providing privacy APIs to address requests from their tenants and potential 3rd parties. The 3rd parties that buy personal information must have their own mechanism to address opt-out and opt-in privacy right - 'do not sell my personal information.' These 3rd parties would save time and resources by providing 2 APIs one for opt-out and another for opt-in.

Now you have a budget, a set of CCPA requirements with priorities, a plan with owners, and a schedule. Next up is to identify critical path tasks, tasks that take more time, and tasks that are likely beyond your budget. You are now ready to get your plan approved by the sponsoring executive.

As a sponsoring executive, you should kick off the project. Also, you should accept that you are unlikely to find a budget needed to complete all the tasks. You should start considering privacy as a competitive advantage. Purely from a compliance angle, you are unlikely to find the budget. This helps you position your business as a responsible player. Beyond privacy laws, you know your users better than they know themselves. Your business needs to address your users' concerns & rights, and build & retain their trust.

Actions:
- Create a project plan.
- Have a list of critical tasks that are beyond your current budget.
- Get the plan approved by sponsoring executive.

Things to Avoid:
- Do not force fit a schedule.

Remember:
- Ownership and accountability are key to project completion on-budget.
- Finish this step in a few days, at most a week.

CHAPTER FIVE

Essential steps

This chapter is about essential steps. Let's revisit what you have done so far.

- Formed a core team (and an extended team),
- Established clear goals,
- Got a budget,
- Prioritized CCPA requirements applicable to your business, and
- Approved a plan for execution.

Your main goals of CCPA compliance are:

a) avoid enforcement action,

b) avoid private action to the extent possible,

c) be on budget, and

d) maintain a schedule.

Now that you have a completed plan, let's get started with execution.

First step - kickoff

Get the core team together. Get key members of the support and operational team together, as well. Clearly state the goals, timeline, and owners. Your program manager takes over, and is now finally accountable to complete the implementation on schedule and in the budget.

Do you already have a designated senior person who is responsible for all your data and its security? Then this person is your IT program owner. For mid-size or small enterprises, this is an operational role. For larger companies, the teams and roles could be wider, and consider splitting this role for data and security.

Resources are precious. So is governance and risk management. It is important to ensure that the decision-makers are informed periodically through the implementation. Establish a process to address escalations. Establish a process to involve legal, IT, security, and other teams where required. This need not be elaborate.

Remember, CCPA is a new law. Its limits have not been tested yet. Your plan is to be ready to mitigate risks. A theme I reiterate in the book – there is no market guidance or established best practice. There is no guidance on the number of privacy requests you can expect. There is no guidance on the number of notices of action (related to private action or notice to AG) from California residents. There is no guidance on penalties and their severity by the Attorney

General of California. However, you need to be ready. Readiness implies fortifying what you already do:

- Be transparent with your privacy and cookie policies.
- Provide a web page for privacy requests (new).
- Ask your partners and service providers the right questions.
- Know your data.
- Be responsible for protecting your data from exfiltration.

Now, you have a small team that has a clear objective. This team has a simple plan. As a sponsoring executive, you could pay attention to these high priority tasks for CCPA compliance.

Task	Priority
Data collection for notices and policy changes	High
Privacy request intake management	High
Website changes and disclosures	High
Inventory of 3rd party sell-to partners	High
Communications plan (external parties)	High
Data security top 20 assessment	High
Email templates for request-response (workflow)	Medium
Inventory of data stores	Medium
New data security initiatives	Medium
Data lookup automation	Medium
Audit, training, governance	Low

The following are additional tasks for software companies, SaaS companies, mobile or web app companies, and service providers.

Task	Priority
Create an API service for data lookup	High
Review data access and storage security (exfiltration risk)	High
Review licensing terms vis-à-vis data privacy provisions	High

Next step – notices, disclosures, and privacy policy

Your business has a website. And you likely have a privacy policy. It is time to review your privacy policy. CCPA is a broad privacy law. The personal information (PI), as discussed earlier, is very broad. It need not be personally identifiable information (PII). It is the right time for your business to review your data collection and use policies.

Earlier, I detailed the privacy policy and its implications. Your privacy notices and disclosures should be simple. One option is to summarize your privacy notice in plain English, and then provide a more legal version of the notice as a secondary disclosure. I recommend you provide appropriate links within your summary, so there is no confusion. Here is an example, for review with your legal and marketing teams:

My Company Privacy Policy

Summary:

- We collect personal information when you use our website (product, service) and other ways. Click here to know all the ways we collect information.
- The categories of information we collect are **click here**.
- The reasons we collect information are **click here**.
- We share/sell your personal information to these **types of companies**.
  - Or: We do not share/sell your personal information
- To stop sale of your personal information, **click here**.
- We honor your privacy rights, **click here** to exercise your privacy rights.
- The information we collect is protected, click here for details.
- Sign up to our list to know of any changes to our policy, click here.

A detailed privacy policy should have the following sections:

- Types of information collected
- Purpose of collection
- Sources of information collection
- How is information shared/sold
- Categories of 3rd party companies you sell-to
- Information protection
- Your rights and choices

- Children and consent
- Changes to policy

Privacy request intake management, data lookup, reasonable security, partner & customer amendments, and a communications plan are discussed in detail in the following chapters.

Actions:

- Kickoff the project with core and extended teams.
- As sponsoring executive focus on fewer high priority tasks.

Things to Avoid:

- Do not rush disclosures, notices, or policy changes.

Remember:

- Document these steps so you could avoid enforcement actions.

CHAPTER SIX

Automate request intake

Privacy Rights Management is one of the key starting elements of CCPA compliance. This applies to nearly all businesses. This helps automate the intake process. A number of vendors provide intake management software. While your business can build intake management software, I strongly recommend buying. It is cheaper and addresses any future regulatory changes.

CCPA privacy requests

Verify request
Automate email verification of privacy request you receive. Add SMS or phone verification, if needed.

STEP 01

STEP 02

Assign request
With automation, a 1-2 person team is sufficient to process all the requests.

Fetch data
Data integration and 3rd party APIs help collate and collect all data needed.

STEP 03

STEP 04

Legal review
For 3 types of requests and exceptions, add legal review process to reduce risk...

Respond
Done! Time to respond to the consumer with email! Keep an audit trail.

STEP 05

A privacy request is a request to execute the right to privacy, as defined in the CCPA. Another term being used is DSAR – data subject access request. Privacy request is a better term because the request is about privacy, including a request for access to data. DSAR is more specific to request for access to personal information. For CCPA compliance, a requestor is a California resident. The privacy requests could be from customers, web site visitors, partners, job applicants, or others. An amendment to the CCPA was signed into law to exempt employees, and contractors from submitting privacy requests. This amendment is likely to expire on Jan 1, 2021. It is unclear if this employee exemption amendment will be made permanent. The types of privacy requests include the following:

- Do not sell my personal information
- Delete my personal information
- Provide my personal information
- Provide my personal information sold
- Give a list of categories of my personal information collected
- Give a list of categories of 3rd parties you sold my data
- Give a list of sources of data collection
- Give a list of reasons for data collection
- Notice of action

The notice of action privacy request is not required under CCPA regulations. I recommend this option to be presented to the consumer. This helps to communicate better with the consumer in case of any infraction by the business. Please consult your legal team.

Deploy

I provided a list of vendors that provide intake management software in the appendix. Evaluate them for your needs and deploy it at your earliest possible. This is the first step in addressing the CCPA compliance. You need to deploy two methods. I recommend:

a) automated web form, and

b) automated 1-800 number

The web intake form must have fields including email (required field), name (optional), phone number (optional), selectable 'type of privacy request' (select one from list above, required), selectable 'Type of requestors' (select one from list above, required), comment (optional), and for web forms a captcha field. The form must have the capability to avoid spam and robot stuffing intake requests. This form with some changes could be used to automate the 1-800-service-number.

I recommend that you include the request types such as collection purposes, data categories, and data sources. Your business may provide this information as part of the disclosure notice. But the reason I make this recommendation is regulatory and to understand your visitors better. Your Chief Marketing Officer will be able to analyze trust levels. He can infer informational requests vs. actionable requests. It is likely that most of your requesters seek assurance on the use of their personal information. Your CMO could deploy a more advanced privacy program and call these requesters and engage them to improve trust and brand value. I also recommend including the notice of the action request. However, consult your legal team and understand the consequences of including notice of action requests.

Verification

The second step of processing a privacy request is verification. The requestor and the request need to be verified. In the request form when you use a captcha, this ensures that no bots are used. There are several ways to verify a requestor and the request.

> During a discussion with one of my customers, I discovered an incorrect understanding of verification as per the CCPA and the regulations. Verification is not on the business collecting personal information, i.e., verify if the business collects personal information. Under CCPA, verification is to 'verify the identity of the consumer making a request.' So in this section, I shall address verification of the identity of the consumer making the requests.

The first method of verification is email verification. This is one of the most widely used and automated processes. Email verification is about ensuring that the email address is valid. This improves the odds that the email address belongs to a real person. The intent of using email verification is to ensure that a real person receives the email sent as part of the privacy request processing.

As part of the email verification process, the privacy request processing system sends a verification email. Another option is to use an email verification service to check on the authenticity of the email address. This ensures that the email is sent, and there are no issues to communicate with the consumer. Also, this means that there are no spelling mistakes by the consumer at the time of the request. Additionally, the domain name is verified. Next up, the requestor reads the verification email and is prompted to click on the link to verify the validity of the email address to proceed with request processing.

The email verification does not specifically verify the authenticity of the name, phone number, or the message of the requestor. But, it is the first step of the process of verifying the privacy request.

The second step of verification is to use SMS or OTP (one-time-password) verification. This requires the consumer's phone number as part of the privacy request intake form. The phone number can easily be verified by sending a text message with verification code or automated voice call with the code. The privacy request system will then ask for the verification code there-in, ensuring that the phone number used by the requestor to present the privacy request is accurate. OTP verification is a widely used technology. However, your requestor may skip this for privacy concerns.

The third step of verification is location verification. Your website visitor's IP address is available in your website analytics tool. You may find ways to identify the IP address. There are several tools or API services that could be used to find the geolocation based on IP address. A more accurate approach would be to include a request for one-time location tracking when the user submits the privacy request. This may be an inaccurate method of location verification. But, this is one way to eliminate requests from outside of California. I recommend that you consider a policy to address all privacy requests without regard to location. Check a recent Microsoft announcement that they plan to support CCPA across the United States (Julie Brill, 2019). This ensures that you are ready for any new CCPA-type laws in other states. See appendix for a list of other states which contemplate new privacy laws.

Other verification mechanisms could include account numbers (credit card number), social security numbers, call-back the consumer to check the authenticity of the request, copy of the utility bill, and more.

I recommend that you start with email verification. You may follow up with a phone call to the consumer in case of delete data, access data, or notice of action requests. Ensure that you have the following rules for request verification:

- CCPA privacy request once received cannot be modified.
- Any privacy request received (data & time) must be verified for requestor identity prior to processing (opt-out of sale does not require verification).
- Email verification is required for communication; SMS phone number verification, verification by phone call, or geolocation verification are good to have.
- ONE verification confirmation is sufficient, while the system or user may request several verifications.
- Requestor verification status and process applies to all types of requests and all types of requestors (exception - opt-out of sale).
- You may assign a request to a request processor before or after request verification.
- Request processor may start work on a request only after request verification is completed.
- Do not send any email notification until the email verification is received.

Email templates

Email notification templates are required for privacy request intake management. This makes your process consistent and scales your request processing. The email template table provided in chapter 3, lists the templates you require for CCPA compliance privacy request processing.

Workflow

Workflow is the key part of processing the CCPA privacy requests. You need to discuss and decide on the workflow, and maintain the status of the workflow. This is a simple process setup. For example, if your business gets over 500 privacy requests a month, then you need 1-3 person team to process these requests. I recommend the following workflow states for your business:

1. Under verification – Implies the request was received and pending verification of the requester.

2. To be assigned – Implies the privacy request process manager is yet to assign the request for processing.

3. Under review – default state once request is verified and assigned.

4. Under legal review – implies that request is sent to the legal approver for review with data or files attached (required only for a few requests).

5. Legal rejected – implies that legal has not approved based on the request and data attached.

6. Legal more information – implies that legal does not have sufficient data to approve the request.

7. Legal approved – implies that request is received from legal as approved.

8. Completed – implies that the requester received an email completing the processing of the request.

9. Rejected – implies that the requester received an email with an explanation of the rejection of the request.

Let's establish a few common elements of processing any of the CCPA privacy requests. As always, consult your legal team. These include:

1. Extend the time needed for processing.

2. Send email notification to the requester (based on templates).

3. Preparation of data – collect and collate the personal information of the requester.

CCPA requires that a request received must be processed within 45 days. The clock starts upon receipt of the request. A good privacy request process helps you process most of the privacy requests within 5 days. CCPA provides you with a way to extend your request processing by an additional 45 days. You need to send the process extension notification to the requester before the expiration of the 45 days of initial processing (to a maximum of 90 days), and with the specific reason for the extension. I recommend you send this process extension email using a standard email template. CCPA allows for one extension. I recommend using the process extension only for 4 types of requests. These include requests for access to personal data, access to data sold or shared, do not sell, and delete data.

The objective of CCPA privacy request processing, is to communicate with the requester. Email is the easiest way to communicate. The requester email must be verified using an email verification process. Additionally, sending emails is inherent to the workflow process. This verification is critical, as sending personal data to the wrong person will be considered a data exfiltration (breach). This is subject to private action by the consumer.

Nearly all CCPA privacy requests require personal data of the consumer, so the request processor can make appropriate response decisions. It is important to ensure that you have the ability to query, collect, and collate all the data associated with the requester. I discussed data collection and collation in the next chapter. For setting up CCPA privacy request processing, you need the data file for the requester. You may use email address, phone number, name, or other search criteria for querying.

You must ensure that your privacy and legal teams are trained to follow this workflow. I recommend that you review the workflow in detail with an extended team. Training is also mandated under CCPA regulations, and request processing should be included as part of training your privacy and legal teams. This also ensures that your privacy request pipeline is processed smoothly and in a timely manner.

Right to know requests

Right to know privacy requests are similar in processing. Each of these privacy requests can be completed in a few steps or actions:

1. Requester verification is completed.

2. Send email acknowledgment to the requester – request received.

3. Optionally, call the requestor to confirm the request.

4. Get requester data for the past 12 months and attach it to the request, so request processor can process the request properly.

5. Review requester data for collection purpose/data categories/data sources (action).

6. Email the requester with an appropriate email template for collection purpose/data categories/data sources (action).

7. Close the request as completed.

Your business has email templates depending on the type of requestor or type of data sources/data categories/data sources/3rd party categories. Alternately, you may have a generic email template for each of the privacy request types. I recommend that your business should have different templates for different types of requesters. Another alternative is to provide generic collection purpose / data sources / data categories information on your website. I recommend specific request processing. This approach provides a way to engage your consumers better.

Actions:

- Select and deploy privacy requests management software.
- Deploy two methods for request intake (web form and 1-800 number).
- Do email verification, and maybe OTP (one time password) verification.
- Complete your email templates.
- Define your workflow for each type of request.

Things to Avoid:

- Do not sign long-term agreements with vendors.
- In-house development may become expensive long term.

Remember:

- Have a flexible workflow that you could improve over time.
- Get your extended team onboard for request processing.

CHAPTER SEVEN

Data, data, and data

A ll privacy requests need requester specific data to process the request to completion. However, the CCPA has specific rights to consumers regarding their personal information. They are privacy request for access to the data, privacy request for access to data sold/shared, 'Do not sell my personal information' – privacy request, and privacy request to delete data. . A request processor needs this data to process the request to completion.

"They say an elephant never forgets, but that was before I had so many passwords, user names and PIN numbers!"

If your business had done GDPR compliance, there is substantial leverage to address these privacy rights. Before I discuss the technologies and tools, let's first address how to process these four types of requests.

Request to access data

A consumer may request access to data twice a year. This data access is similar to free credit report under FCRA. The CCPA privacy request for access to personal information can be completed in several steps:

1. Complete consumer verification

2. Send email acknowledgment to the requester

3. Call the requestor (optional) to confirm the request

4. Check if this is a valid request

5. Check if a similar request was received from the **same requester in the past 12 months**

    a. You are required to process a request every 6 months. This could imply that you could process 2 requests every 12 months. I recommend that your business keeps track of the number of requests received from a specific consumer. And track processing several types of requests, including the request for access to data, request to delete data, request to access data shared/sold, or request not to sell data.

    b. If one of these types of requests was received in the past 12 months, the business might send a notification to the requester that more than 2 requests were processed in the past 12 months.

    c. If the number of requests is in order, then continue with the next steps.

6. Get requester data for the past 12 months and attach it to the request

7. Review requester data and note any abnormal patterns (action)

8. Send the request including the data and the notes for **legal review** (action)

9. Get approval from the legal reviewer

10. Email the requester with the right email template for access to personal data, and attach the data approved by a legal reviewer

11. Close the request as completed

Your business may have several different email templates for personal information access. Or, you may also have one generic email template. I recommend different templates for different types of requesters. Let's assume that the request processors have a way to look up the data for the specific consumer across all your data stores.

Personal information access is a very tricky area. The CCPA has expanded the definition beyond personally identifiable information. For example, if a visitor to your company website requests data, then it is imperative that you collate all the website statistics for this specific visitor. Website statistics collected by most companies do not have any personally identifiable information. However, under CCPA, it is personal information associated with a cookie ID of the visitor.

Request for data sold/shared

The CCPA privacy request for access to personal information that is sold or shared, is similar to the privacy request for personal information access discussed in the section above. The only difference is in the collation of data from multiple data stores of the company. Your business must have a way to quickly identify if this data is licensed to a third party. CCPA does not require you to share who the data is licensed/sold/shared with. It is unclear if data hosted with a third-party service provider is considered to be part of data shared/licensed. I recommend that hosting data with a third-party service provider, need not be considered as part of this privacy request. Please seek appropriate legal advice.

Request for 'do not sell my personal information'

The CCPA privacy request for **do not sell my personal information** is somewhat similar to the privacy request for personal information access, discussed in the section above. There are a few differences:

1. Do not attach the data collated as part of the response to the requester.

2. Identify a way to mark the data as not for sale and the date of the request in your systems.

3. What if the data was already sold?

    a. There is a need for the company to inform the 3rd parties that received the data

    b. You must acknowledge to the customer that other 3rd parties are informed of their request

4. At the end of 12 months from the date of this type of request, you may sell/share this data. CCPA does not specify any limitations. And please seek appropriate legal advice.

As a special treatment to this type of request, verification has been waived in the regulations from the AG. So the request, whether verified or not, must be treated as valid and processed. However, if your business believes that they received a fraudulent request, then you may reject the request with a reason for rejection. Investing in fraud detection is expensive. So, unless you believe that your competitor or a Nigerian scam artist is stuffing these requests, it is easier to process the request. One approach to detect fraud is by comparing overall % of requests verified vs. % the 'do not sell' requests.

Request for delete data

The CCPA privacy request for **delete my personal information** is somewhat similar to the privacy request for personal information access discussed in the section above. There are a few differences:

1. Controversial: I interpret that a request to delete data does not imply that the consumer is able to opt-out of data collection. You may continue data collection from various sources, post-processing the deletion request. I mark this as controversial because of intent vs. action. In my opinion, the lawmakers did not provide a right to opt-out (or opt-in) of information collection (while GDPR expressly has an opt-in to collection). California tech economy needs this data and the ability to collect this data. So, as a business you may interpret this request as 'delete data collected thus far' and keep collection data from now forward.

2. You may decide to keep some data that is necessary to service the consumer. For example, invoice or payment information may not be deleted. You may need that customer information for returns processing.

3. Do not attach the data collated as part of the response to the requester.

4. Identify a way to mark the data as request for data deletion. I will discuss the tools for deletion later in this chapter.

5. As part of your request processing system, you may retain a copy of the data only for the purpose of a compliance audit.

6. What if the data was already sold? While regulations are unclear on this, I recommend the same treatment as opt-out of sale request

   a. There is a need for the company to inform the 3rd parties that received the data

   b. You must acknowledge to the customer that other 3rd parties are informed of their request

An area of concern using vendor software for privacy request intake management is email responses. Email processing and responses to consumers are sent from the software vendor. This implies this personal information is now stored and processed with this new vendor (i.e. email provider). If the vendor uses their 3rd party cloud transactional email service such as Sendgrid, Amazon SES,

Mandrill, or other, then the response data is stored in those services. Two evaluation criteria you must consider in this situation are: a) does the vendor have the ability to send emails using custom domain email address, and b) does the vendor delete data from transactional email services.

Privacy APIs and data lookup

For any automated or manual data lookup your business needs to create an inventory of data assets. Leverage the inventory of your IT systems that you may already have. Your compliance implementation should initially focus on a manual process to query and fetch data from all your data assets. I emphasize a manual process as a first step because you will have clarity of definition of personal information stored in your systems not simply personally identifiable information. The query is to be based on the consumer's email address, phone number, name, or a combination of these. This manual process is expensive and time-consuming, but necessary.

Based on the manual process, you have clarity of which queries to implement and data to be fetched. Now you could start the process of automating these queries. You may quickly automate the data lookup and fetch. Once the data is received in your request management system, a request processor should have the capability to edit or mask pieces of data. The CCPA regulations state that your business shall not provide specific pieces of information that creates unreasonable risk to the security of the information.

"A business shall not provide a consumer with specific pieces of personal information if the disclosure creates a substantial, articulable, and unreasonable risk to the security of that personal information, the consumer's account with the business, or the security of the business's systems or networks.

A business shall not at any time disclose a consumer's Social Security number, driver's license number or other government-issued identification number, financial account number, any health insurance or medical identification number, an account password, or security questions and answers." – CCPA Regulations from Attorney General (California A. G.).

For example, when you receive personal information stored from your payment processing microservice or cloud provider, either the payment processing masks the information or your request processor masks the credit card or security code information.

The following list helps automate your data lookup and processing.

1. Look up data by consumer email, consumer phone number, or both

2. Look up data sold by consumer email, consumer phone number, or both

3. Execute opt-out of sale by consumer email, consumer phone number; or both

4. Execute opt-in to sale by consumer email, consumer phone number; or both

5. Execute delete data of consumer by consumer email, consumer phone number, or both

There is no specific tool or vendor that provides the privacy API look up mechanism. But this could be built out of your current API management systems. This automation of data lookup is a time-consuming process. You may consider automation if the number of requests exceeds 100 requests per month. This implies a budget of $150K to $300K in annual personnel, costs depending on the number of data stores. This annual budget requires you to deploy privacy API data lookup automation.

If you are a service provider or a SaaS business, I strongly recommend implementing privacy APIs. Your customers could fetch all the personal information store in your cloud or service. The format could be a JSON CLOB (character large object). The response to requesting consumer must be human readable.

Vendors addressing CCPA compliance pitch data mapping as the first step. I do not recommend this. If your IT team has a fairly complete inventory, you do not need other tools to map your data. Data mapping tools do not provide a way to access the data. They are used to inventory your assets. They can also be used to manually identify data flows.

Data discovery (or eDiscovery) helps you identify and classify structured, unstructured, and semi-structured data. This is a required tool for PCI, HIPAA, and other compliance. Traditionally, data discovery tools do not provide a way to access the data. However, a few data discovery tools have recently started to provide data lookup functionality as well. Please evaluate the data discovery tools for this purpose. Consider the ability of the data discovery tools to query based on the privacy request. For example, correlation of email ID of the requester with cookie ID in analytics data. This correlation may not be possible with data discovery tools, unless the tool provides an ability to declare proximity as a search criterion. Additionally, data discovery tools may not deliver a full scan in a reasonable timeframe. Each scan may require extensive processing capabilities or additional processing licenses from vendors. Another issue to consider is data staging by data discovery vendors. Staged data creates another data asset location to address privacy request processing. You need to ensure all staged data is temporary.

Agreements, amendments

CCPA holds you responsible for all the personal information you collect/buy/share. You may share or store or license to external parties. It is now necessary that the external parties treat this personal information under CCPA compliance. This third party

CCPA compliance implies your external parties need to answer the following questions:

1. Can you process opt-out requests – Do Not Sell My Personal Information?

2. Do you have tools to identify, monitor, and delete personal information?

3. How do you encrypt personal information or anonymize it?

4. Do you have a process to detect and respond to data breaches?

Nearly all service providers need to get ready for CCPA compliance. Data brokers or data as service companies, need to register themselves with the California AG and address CCPA. CCPA compliance may not apply to smaller business partners. However, encouraging all your business partners ensures that your business has protection from liability. Execute an amendment to your current agreement with each of the 3rd party partners. I recommend the following clause in your amendment.

Covenant to Safeguard Personal Information and CCPA compliance.

(a) Covenant. Company (3rd party vendor) and any affiliate of the Company, each covenant to safeguard Personal Information (as defined in CCPA California Consumer Privacy Act – AB 375), and to institute a reasonable procedure, practice, or technology that safeguards Personal

Information, from any digital means (not limiting to personal, network, or cloud means) used by the Company, any subsidiary, any affiliate, or any employee of the Company.

(b) Data breach or attempt to steal by a person(s) or machines or bot(s). This covenant shall include data breach prevention from any or all thefts or attempts to steal by a person(s), machine(s), bot(s), or a combination thereof.

(c) Report data breaches, attempts. The Company shall provide periodic reports, no longer than each six (6) months of the data breach incident, or an attempt to steal any or all Personal Information. The incident report of a data breach or attempt to steal such Personal Information shall at the minimum, include data and time of the incident, the location of the incident, details of specific Personal Information involved in the incident, the person(s) or bot(s) responsible for the incident, among other information related to the incident. At the discretion of the Company, any data breach or attempt to steal highly confidential information shall be reported immediately.

(d) Privacy APIs and CCPA Compliance. The Company shall institute a procedure, practice, or technology that addresses privacy requests. These include, but not limited to access to personal information (a minimum of two times a year per consumer), acknowledgment to delete specific personal information, acknowledgment to stop sale (or license) of specific personal information to other 3rd parties.

I also recommend that your business execute a similar clause in your terms of service with your customers. This will enhance trust and your relationship with your customers. Such amendments are highly useful with large business partners.

Actions:

- Create an inventory of data stores.
- Test your data lookup procedure.
- Execute amendments with your partners, vendors, 3rd parties (sell-to).

Things to Avoid:

- Do not execute amendments all at once, be selective.

Remember:

- These activities will take a lot of time beyond the California AG deadline.
- Get started, and you can avoid enforcement action.

CHAPTER EIGHT

Reasonable security

Data security is another key part of privacy. Remember, privacy does not imply security. Privacy is about policies on how you treat data, its risk, governance, and compliance. Security is about protecting personal information from unauthorized access. Security as part of CCPA compliance can be broken into three areas:

a. reasonable security procedures,

b. encryption, hashing, tokenization or data protection, and

c. anonymization or pseudonymization as part of data deletion requests.

Reasonable security measures

I discussed that one of our goals is to avoid private action. In the event of a data breach, class-action is seen as inevitable. The CCPA is clear on the action – 'implement and maintain reasonable security procedures and practices.'

AB 375 (Legislature A. 3., 2018) - #1798.150

(a) (1) Any consumer whose nonencrypted or nonredacted personal information, as defined in subparagraph (A) of paragraph (1) of subdivision (d) of Section 1798.81.5, is subject to an unauthorized access and exfiltration, theft, or disclosure as a result of the business' violation of the duty to implement and maintain reasonable security procedures and practices, appropriate to the nature of the information to protect the personal information, may institute a civil action for any of the following:

(A) To recover damages in an amount not less than one hundred dollars ($100) and not greater than seven hundred and fifty ($750) per consumer per incident or actual damages, whichever is greater.

(B) Injunctive or declaratory relief.

(C) Any other relief the court deems proper.

As discussed in chapter 3, the SANS top 20 security controls are now interpreted as the Center for Internet Security's (CIS) critical security controls. Addressing these CIS 20 is often considered industry best practice, and can be interpreted as reasonable security procedures. Implementing these controls may not avoid data breaches or subsequent plaintiff class-actions. However, not implementing these may be interpreted as lack of reasonable security. Here is the list that you may reference (CISecurity).

CSC 1: Inventory of Authorized and Unauthorized Devices
CSC 2: Inventory of Authorized and Unauthorized Software
CSC 3: Secure Configurations for Hardware and Software on Mobile Devices, Laptops, Workstations, and Servers
CSC 4: Continuous Vulnerability Assessment and Remediation
CSC 5: Controlled Use of Administrative Privileges
CSC 6: Maintenance, Monitoring, and Analysis of Audit Logs
CSC 7: Email and Web Browser Protections
CSC 8: Malware Defenses
CSC 9: Limitation and Control of Network Ports, Protocols and Services
CSC 10: Data Recovery Capability
CSC 11: Secure Configurations for Network Devices, such as Firewalls, Routers, and Switches
CSC 12: Boundary Defense
CSC 13: Data Protection
CSC 14: Controlled Access Based on the Need to Know
CSC 15: Wireless Access Control
CSC 16: Account Monitoring and Control
CSC 17: Security Skills Assessment and Appropriate Training to Fill Gaps
CSC 18: Application Software Security
CSC 19: Incident Response and Management
CSC 20: Penetration Tests and Red Team Exercises

The action is an annual assessment of your business' security procedures against these CIS 20 security controls. I recommend a 3rd party assessment. This ensures that you are following a process, and you are methodical in your action to implement and maintain reasonable security procedures.

As a security expert, I know this assessment can go long and wide. And a detailed assessment can eat away all your budget. I recommend doing a simple and quick assessment to point out the glaring holes in your security procedures. In addition to that, look in-depth in Data Protection or data theft prevention using DLP products, or simply encrypting the data.

Data theft prevention

One of the SANS top 20 recommendations is data protection. Deploying DLP or data loss prevention products is one way to prevent theft of personal information. Gartner's research estimates that nearly 90% of enterprises would have implemented at least one form of DLP. Another way to protect personal information and avoid private action under CCPA is to encrypt personal information.

There are three areas of DLP deployment:

    a) end-points (such as laptops, mobile devices, and computers)

    b) network, and

c) cloud apps such as Office 365

Some vendors provide all three solutions as an integrated package. However, each type of deployment has multiple vendors. End-point DLP is similar to deploying an anti-virus or anti-malware application on your computer. After you address the end-point, it is time to pay attention to your network. Your business needs the ability to proxy, classify, and prevent any unauthorized exfiltration (breach). Evaluate and engage your vendors regarding malicious insider exfiltration of data. It is one of the most difficult problems to solve. Benefits of network data loss prevention include:

- Control traffic on email, HTTP(S), (s)FTP, webmail, web apps, and more
- Control clear as well as SSL based applications
- Enforce policies
- Reduce false positive
- Prevent insider threats as well as threats from bots
- Provide forensics where required

Now that you took care of your end-points and network, it is time to pay attention to your cloud applications. Office 365 is one of the most widely used applications. Deploying end-point DLP and network DLP is not sufficient to prevent exfiltration (breach) from Office 365. Why? It is because Office 365 is a cloud application and can be accessed using uncontrolled end-points. So, I recommend deploying Office 365 DLP and choose a vendor that supports multiple cloud applications. I added a list of DLP vendors in the appendix for your reference.

Data encryption

The alternative to deploying a DLP solution is to encrypt data. Similar to the DLP solution, encryption solution should also be deployed in multiple locations – your end-points, your network, and your cloud applications. Your data (personal information) could be at rest stored in application or web servers, file servers, databases, network-attached storage devices, or backup devices. Your data (personal information) is also vulnerable as it moves across your network or over the internet.

Data encryption solutions need to address authorized access and secure any unauthorized access to data. This data could be structured data, resting in databases, or unstructured data resting in file servers. To avoid man-in-the-middle theft, data-in-motion also needs to be encrypted. When users need the data for any authorized purpose, this data needs to be decrypted. For encryption or decryption, keys are critical. And if the keys are vulnerable, then the encryption is useless. As a result, one big issue with encryption solutions is key storage. To keep keys safe, they are stored securely, and the keys are not distributed. This implies that encryption and decryption need to be done at a place where the keys are stored. This is typically called a hair-pinning problem. It results in network latencies and slow processing. I believe distributed encryption and decryption do solve the problem of network speeds and processing.

At times, your cloud infrastructure may not be in your control, and you may have to depend on your vendors to safeguard your digital assets. First, I recommend that you execute appropriate amendments to safeguard your data. Next step is vendor evaluation for key management. Some vendors provide you with the ability to use your own keys for encryption and decryption of your personal information in their cloud infrastructure.

Explore all your options. You need to evaluate which solution is more effective for your business. CCPA compliance should not be the key driver in selecting and deploying either a DLP or encryption solution. Your security posture and an overall need to protect your digital assets should drive these deployments. I state this primarily from the perspective of budgets. The data security budget, in response to CCPA compliance, should be from an existing pool of resources, there-in reducing the burden to find new data security resources for CCPA compliance. Alternately, CCPA compliance may require action from your Board to approve additional resources for data security.

Anonymization or data deletion

The main purpose of anonymization is to delete personal information of the requesting consumer effectively. This method of data deletion in response to the request to delete data, is appropriate as part of CCPA compliance. A key condition of anonymization for CCPA compliance is to ensure that the data cannot be re-identified. Anonymization is done using several techniques such as attribute suppression, record suppression, and character masking.

CCPA compliance for delete requests can also be accomplished effectively by encrypting the specific consumers' personal information with a random key and then deleting the key from all records. But this type of anonymization will lose the analytical value of the data. And as such, this may not be a preferred approach for some businesses.

Another technique called pseudonymization may also be used for this purpose. This technique effectively replaces the personal information, identifying information with randomly generated made-up values. I recommend using irreversible pseudonymization, so the original values are disposed, and the process is irreversible. One way to achieve this, is to have a fairly large library of a set of values for the personally identifiable values in your data. Once you receive a delete request, then replace the consumer personal information with one of these randomly selected values from the library.

Actions:

- Get a quick and dirty security assessment.
- Deploy a DLP system.
- Deploy a anonymization tool for your delete data requests.

Things to Avoid:

- Do not go overboard with your security assessment.

Remember:

- Not enough budget for security, go to the Board.
- Annual security assessments.
- Test the random nature of your anonymization tool.

CHAPTER NINE

Communications plan

Acommunication plan for CCPA compliance goes beyond internal team communication. In this chapter, I shall address a plan to ensure that it drives the completion of your CCPA compliance. Your communication plan needs to include:

- Deployment of appropriate content and disclosure on your website
- Responses to consumer requests
- Amendments and change notices to B2B customers, partners, vendors, etc.
- Amendments and privacy API requests to companies you sell/share personal information

Website

CCPA compliance needs changes to the website. You also need to deploy privacy requests management software and web forms. Disclosures, changes to terms and policy changes also need to be deployed. I detailed these changes in chapter 5.

As part of the communication plan, you need to ensure that each of these changes is consistent:

- Maintain your company branding and style,
- Maintain simplicity in your message,
- When creating an email response template, include the privacy link,
- Provide right contact information (include the privacy link), and
- When sending SMS messages, include the privacy link.

What	Who	When	How
Privacy policy, terms	Web user	Jan 1, 2020	Change website
Disclosures	Web user	Jan 1, 2020	Change website
Do Not Sell Button	Web user	Jan 1, 2020	Change website
1-800 number (privacy request)	Web user	Jan 1, 2020	Change website
Web form (privacy request)	Web user	Jan 1, 2020	Change website
Policy changes	Employees	Jan 1, 2020	Email (refer website)

Responses to consumers

Privacy request intake management requires email verification, acknowledgment by email, and more. Follow some simple guidelines to create these templates, discussed in chapters 3 and 6.

What	Who	When	How
Email responses	Consumer	Ongoing	Email templates
1-800 number responses	Consumer	Ongoing	Email templates
OTP messages	Consumer	Ongoing	SMS with policy link
Verification calls	Consumer	Ongoing	Phone calls

Customers (B2B)

CCPA compliance and policy changes require notices to customers. This may also require changes to the terms of service. Another potential requirement could be amendments to current agreements. Your business must address all of the above in an organized fashion.

What	Who	When	How
Policy & terms changes/ Amendments	Sales teams	Jan-Jul 2020	Training/Sales Decks
Amendments	Customer	Jan-Jul 2020	Emails, calls, sales
Changes to terms of service	Customer	Jan-Jul 2020	Email
Policy change notices	Customer	Jan-Jul 2020	Email
Terms and policy changes	Account-holders	Upon login	Display pop-ups

Partners / vendors / service providers

Similar to B2B customers, CCPA compliance and policy changes require notices to partners, vendors, and service providers. Similar to your customers, you may have to amend your current agreements with your partners. This table provides a guideline to address these items.

What	Who	When	How
Policy & terms changes /Amendments	Internal teams	Jan-Jul 2020	Training
Amendments	Vendors	Jan-Jul 2020	Emails, calls, sales
Amendments	Service providers	Jan-Jul 2020	Emails, calls, sales
Policy & terms changes /Amendments	Partners	Jan-Jul 2020	Emails, calls, sales
Privacy API requests	Service providers	Jan-Jul 2020	Calls, meetings
Privacy API requests	Vendors	Jan-Jul 2020	Calls, meetings

3rdparty (sell-to) companies

If your business sells/shares personal information with 3rd party companies, then you must consider a more hands on approach to communicate your privacy policies. You need them to provide an API for the intake of do not sell and delete data requests.

What	Who	When	How
Privacy API calls	Internal IT team	Jan-Jul 2020	Training, meetings
Amendments	3rd party	Jan-Jul 2020	Emails, calls, sales
Policy & terms changes notices	3rd party	Jan-Jul 2020	Emails
Privacy API requests intake	3d party	Jan-Jul 2020	Calls, meetings

Actions:

- Create a detailed communication plan.
- Have an owner for smooth, consistent communication.
- Get the plan approved by sponsoring executive.

Things to Avoid:

- Do not fret about the schedule.

Remember:

- This is a long process and is likely to take a long time to complete.
- Be persistent.

Continued compliance

I believe having done all the steps I recommended above, you would have achieved your key goals:

a) Reach CCPA compliance,

b) Avoid enforcement action, and

c) Avoid private action.

"The usual stuff — a new virus from the Joker, spyware from the Penguin, malicious code from Cat Woman, another phishing scheme from the Riddler."

The key question remaining is, what steps you need to take to ensure easy ongoing compliance with the CCPA. I recommend ongoing activities detailed in this chapter.

Contracts and agreements

The first step to continued compliance is to ensure that you change your template agreements to reflect your new privacy policy and the realities of CCPA compliance. You had previously changed your terms of service and privacy policy. You also executed amendments with your partners, customers, vendors, 3rd parties, and service providers. It is time to incorporate these changes into your template agreements. This will help you and your team to engage new vendors, customers, service providers, and other external parties with the right privacy clauses in the agreements.

Training

Training is a compliance requirement, and it is key to ensure that your team understands the privacy law, the regulations, and their responsibilities. Training is more important for privacy request processors. These privacy request processors need to handle all the requests from consumers. As discussed earlier, one key area for request processors is to ensure that information disclosed to consumers as part of the request processing does not create a security risk. Ongoing training also helps with any policy changes, and new amendments to the law or regulations.

IAPP and several other privacy organizations offer privacy training. I believe they are likely to offer CCPA specific privacy training as well. Several privacy consulting firms also offer such training. This training must be combined with your business' specific privacy policies, privacy request workflow, and your data lookup mechanisms. Additionally, your IT and security staff need training on data breach incident response and management. I assume you incident response program is funded under your security budget.

Documentation

You spent all the effort, resources, and budget to get to CCPA compliance. It is important to document the effort and changes. This ensures that you have documentation when the California AG knocks on your door with an enforcement action. Documentation may also reflect the changes you have made for securing and processing personal information. I recommend that you conduct an annual documentation review and update.

Risk management

I believe you conduct a periodic risk assessment, potentially an annual risk assessment. This is a good business practice. Add CCPA compliance to that risk assessment activities. Actively managing risk or periodically doing risk assessment requires that you review workflows, systems, and vendor relationships. This is likely to identify risks in privacy request processing. This process helps in changing the process and mitigate serious risks in CCPA compliance.

Another area of risk is private action. Mitigating a data breach risk requires that you perform a more periodic data protection impact assessment. I recommend using a red team approach once a quarter, to perform this data protection assessment. Additionally, this helps improve your cybersecurity risk management, as well.

Cyber liability insurance

I intentionally did not discuss cyber liability insurance in this book, because it is related to risk management and not compliance. However, I do feel it is important to mention it. You made a big investment, and are committing to an additional annual investment for CCPA compliance. The CCPA also has a big impact on cyber insurance.

In many cyber insurance policies today, privacy data is narrowly defined as personally identifiable data. Personal information definition under the CCPA substantially expands the foundational risk coverage of most cyber policies. The expansion of scope of covered data, obviously expands the number of claims under the privacy policy. Your insurance premiums may go up.

A more significant issue with most cyber policies is private action. This implies 3rd party claims. Thus far, awards are minimal to none resulting from data breach plaintiff actions. I recommend that you thoroughly review your cyber insurance policy. Do you have a stand-alone cyber policy or an endorsement? Does your policy address the new definition of personal information? Does your policy have an exception for gathering and distribution of data? Engage your insurer to check on your coverage for CCPA.

Service provider / vendor risk management

You created a CCPA compliance amendment for execution by each vendor or service provider. It is likely that you are able to get 80% of your vendors to sign this amendment. However, this is not enough. There is still a risk of penalties or class-action lawsuits. It is an operational risk. The vendor has likely executed the amendment. Is there a way to check their CCPA compliance? This is the tough part. So, you need a vendor risk assessment. There are two areas of vendor risk assessment for CCPA.

1. *Vendor security risk assessment.* How vulnerable is the vendor for data breaches? Making this assessment on a vendor is a difficult operational problem. You may seek a periodic vulnerability assessment report from your vendors. You could negotiate this in your agreements, provided that you have a negotiating leverage.

2. *Vendor privacy request compliance assessment.* How well does the vendor comply with the request for personal information? How well does the vendor comply with the request for the deletion of data? How well does the vendor comply with the request not to sell personal information? This assessment is

easier. Check your request intake management to verify vendor compliance.

Several companies offer services to make a 3rd party vendor security assessment for GDPR compliance. The market is still evolving. I referenced a list of resources that provide a vendor risk assessment for GDPR compliance in the appendix. This could be easily extended to CCPA compliance.

Privacy request workflow review

You now have a program that is working. You could make periodic improvements to reduce costs or improve effectiveness. Many businesses are likely still working on getting their CCPA compliance programs off the ground. You could take it further to improve your program. One key area of improvement would be automating data lookup, and there in automating several right to know requests.

Actions:

- Train your internal teams periodically as other states embraces CCPA-like laws.
- Do an annual compliance audit.
- Change your main agreements to reflect new privacy policy.
- Keep your sponsors in the loop on improvements.

Things to Avoid:

- Do not overthink compliance, it should be part of enforcing your privacy policy.

Remember:

- Avoid enforcement action.
- Avoid private action.

CHAPTER LAST

Summary

It is time to summarize. You bought this book to get CCPA compliance. You now have the knowledge and the focus to take on this new privacy regulation. I firmly believe that you will also be ready for any CCPA like regulations in the works in several states. Let's identify the value you got out of paying for, and spending the time reading this book:

1. You determine if your company needs to be ready for CCPA compliance

   a. Effective date – January 1, 2020

   b. Date of enforcement start – July 1, 2020

2. You have clear goals

   a. Avoid enforcement action

   b. Avoid private action

3. You have a preliminary budget and a team

4. Your team identified the requirements and marked up the priority

5. Your team created a plan, ownership, and a schedule

6. Your team then implemented changes to the website

    a. Privacy request intake

    b. Policy notices and disclosures

7. You looked into data lookup and identified ways to process key privacy requests

    a. Data, data, data

    b. You implemented a manual data lookup process

    c. You may not have complete data lookup automation, but you got started

8. You then rolled up your sleeve about security and avoiding private action

    a. You do not have a one-pill to chill approach

    b. You have a periodic mechanism to improve your security

    c. You documented your security practices

    d. You keep assessing the risk of private action

9. You have a communication plan to inform all your stakeholders

a. Get everyone on the same page

10. Lastly, you have the tools to do ongoing compliance checks and changes

---

Actions:

- Give this copy of your book to your team lead.
- Get the right people in your business involved.
- Guide your team and let them execute their plan.

Things to Avoid:

- Do not try to control scope, schedule, and budget.

Remember:

- You only have control over the budget.
- Guide your team on how to use the budget for high priority tasks.

Resources

<u>Your comments, ideas, suggestions, and changes</u>

Was this book useful? Did you learn something new? Could you please write a review of my book at Amazon? I'd appreciate it. Is there something I should add? Do you want a new topic to get covered in this book? Do you know of any tool or technique or interesting way to get CCPA compliance done? Send an email.

Sign up for my newsletter so I can let you know when there's an updated version or new books. Subscribe at https://InfoSecEnforcer .com/The-CCPA-Book-NewsLetter

<u>Webpage for this book:</u> https://InfoSecEnforcer.com/The-CCPA-Compliance-Book

<u>Contact DV Dronamraju</u>

Questions or advice? Just ask.

Website: https://InfoSecEnforcer.com

Email: dv@InfoSecEnforcer.com

Blog: https://InfoSecEnforcer.com/ccpa-compliance-resources/

Twitter: @nodatabreach

References

Amnesia. (n.d.). *https://amnesia.openaire.eu/* .

Anonimatron. (n.d.). Retrieved from
     https://realrolfje.github.io/anonimatron/

Apple. (2019). *Apple Privacy*. Retrieved from
     https://www.apple.com/privacy/ .

ARX Data. (n.d.). *https://arx.deidentifier.org/* .

California, A. (n.d.). *CCPA STD399*. Retrieved from
     https://oag.ca.gov/sites/all/files/agweb/pdfs/privacy/ccpa-
     std399.pdf

California, A. G. (n.d.). *CCPA Proposed Regulations*. Retrieved from
     https://www.oag.ca.gov/sites/all/files/agweb/pdfs/privacy/
     ccpa-proposed-regs.pdf

CISecurity. (n.d.). Retrieved from
     https://www.cisecurity.org/controls/

CNBC, Lauren Feiner. (2019). *CNBC*. Retrieved from
     https://www.cnbc.com/2019/10/05/california-consumer-
     privacy-act-ccpa-could-cost-companies-55-billion.html

EU. (2016). *GDPR Text*. Retrieved from https://gdpr-info.eu/ .

IAPP. (2019). *https://iapp.org/resources/article/2019-privacy-tech-
     vendor-report/* .

IAPP. (n.d.). *Data processing addendum.* Retrieved from
https://iapp.org/news/a/a-data-processing-addendum-for-the-ccpa/

Julie Brill. (2019). *Microsoft Corporation.* Retrieved from
https://blogs.microsoft.com/on-the-issues/2019/11/11/microsoft-california-privacy-rights/

Legislature, 2. (n.d.). *AB 25 CCPA.* Retrieved from
https://leginfo.legislature.ca.gov/faces/billTextClient.xhtml?bill_id=201920200AB25

Legislature, A. 3. (2018). *AB 375 California Legislature.* Retrieved from
https://leginfo.legislature.ca.gov/faces/billTextClient.xhtml?bill_id=201720180AB375

Legislature, C. (n.d.). *AB 1130 CCPA.* Retrieved from
https://leginfo.legislature.ca.gov/faces/billTextClient.xhtml?bill_id=201920200AB1130

Legislature, C. (n.d.). *AB 1146 CCPA.* Retrieved from
https://leginfo.legislature.ca.gov/faces/billTextClient.xhtml?bill_id=201920200AB1146

Legislature, C. (n.d.). *AB 1202 CCPA.* Retrieved from
https://leginfo.legislature.ca.gov/faces/billTextClient.xhtml?bill_id=201920200AB1202

Legislature, C. (n.d.). *AB 1355 CCPA.* Retrieved from
https://leginfo.legislature.ca.gov/faces/billTextClient.xhtml?bill_id=201920200AB1355

Legislature, C. (n.d.). *AB 1564 CCPA*. Retrieved from
https://leginfo.legislature.ca.gov/faces/billTextClient.xhtml?
bill_id=201920200AB1564

Legislature, C. (n.d.). *AB 874 CCPA*. Retrieved from
https://leginfo.legislature.ca.gov/faces/billTextClient.xhtml?
bill_id=201920200AB874

Mu. (n.d.). *http://neon.vb.cbs.nl/casc/mu.htm* .

sdcMicro. (n.d.). Retrieved from https://cran.r-
project.org/package=sdcMicro

Settlement, F. (n.d.). Retrieved from
https://www.ftc.gov/enforcement/cases-
proceedings/refunds/equifax-data-breach-settlement

Settlement, F. F. (n.d.). Retrieved from
https://www.ftc.gov/news-events/blogs/business-
blog/2019/07/ftcs-5-billion-facebook-settlement-record-
breaking-history

Zuckerberg, M. (2019). *Privacy Manifesto*. Retrieved from
https://www.facebook.com/notes/mark-zuckerberg/a-
privacy-focused-vision-for-social-
networking/10156700570096634/ .

Appendix

Understand the CCPA terms

I decided to place this in the appendix. I assume some basic knowledge of privacy and law for most of my audience. However, for complete beginners, this section will bring them up to speed. So, let's get on the same page with the terms associated with CCPA.

Personal Information

Personal information is broadly defined under the CCPA. It is information that identifies, relates to, describes, is capable of being associated with, or could reasonably be linked, directly or indirectly, with a particular consumer. Additionally, household data is also included as part of Personal information. This household data need not be about a single person. Personal information should not be confused with personally identifiable information. Personal information is more than personally identifiable information.

You could de-identify the data, and that is exempted from being called Personal information. Any data that cannot be linked directly or indirectly to a specific consumer or household is exempted. And data that is de-identified must not be re-identified. Most privacy laws considered personally identifiable information as a basis for privacy. The CCPA is different in that respect.

Consumer

A consumer under CCPA is a California resident. So, if you are a business engaged in selling to businesses (b2b), CCPA applies. Your customers, partners, and website visitors could potentially be California residents. One exception is a temporary California resident. There is a generic presumption that a person who stays 180 days or more in a year, in California is considered a California resident.

This definition of 'consumer' extends beyond the state borders and is rather difficult to verify. Let's discuss an example. The CCPA applies to California residents who are traveling in Las Vegas. ABC Gaming Company in Las Vegas, NV. It has many customers from California periodically, and the company has over $25 Million in revenue. Either the company or its parent does business in California by obtaining a certificate of qualification. In my opinion, it is better for the ABC Gaming Company to do the minimum required for CCPA compliance.

Business

California Consumer Privacy Act (CCPA) applies only to a selected number of businesses. It applies to business entities that collect consumer personal information. Additionally, an entity conducts business in the State of California, and one of these conditions apply:

1. Earns annual gross revenues in excess of $25,000,000;

2. Buys, receives for commercial purposes, sells, or shares for commercial purposes, the personal information of 50,000 or more consumers, households, or devices per year; or

3. Derives 50 percent or more of its annual revenues from selling consumers' personal information.

Let's discuss an example. ABC Company distributes web and mobile apps. It has 25,000 customers. Each of these customers uses the app on their mobile device and their computer. And the company, as part of the web and mobile app, collects data from all these devices. The purpose of data collection is for product support, product improvement, and/or commercial transactions. Company ABC does not sell or share any personal information with 3rd parties. In this example, CCPA applies to ABC Company. It applies because it receives personal information of 50,000 devices.

Service Provider

The CCPA applies to nearly all service providers. It applies to all service providers that process personal information on behalf of a business. Most service providers have terms of service. As part of CCPA, one of these terms must say that the service provider will not cross-license the personal information collected on behalf of one customer, with another customer or third party.

The CCPA also indicates that a service provider may get a privacy request directly from a consumer. Such a request must be processed, even if that processing includes pointing the consumer to the appropriate business that owns the consumer data. This requirement gets very tricky for the service provider, as discussed in the book.

Let's discuss an example. ABC Company uses Google Analytics on its website and its mobile app. Google Analytics (Google/Alphabet) is a Service Provider. Google Analytics in its terms and conditions, states that it does not share data collected on behalf of ABC Company with any other customer or 3rd party, unless Google Analytics is given explicit permission to do so. However, Google Analytics may use the information in aggregate. As part of CCPA, Google Analytics must comply with the privacy requests from ABC Company on behalf of the consumer.

Third Parties

As a part of the CCPA, a Third Party may be a business or individual. Such Third Party is not a Service Provider, as defined above.

Again, let's discuss an example. ABC Company sells or shares personal information with several other companies or individuals. These companies and individuals are considered to be third parties. They are not Service Providers that are governed by a contract consistent with the CCPA. Other companies may sell or share personal information with ABC Company. Then ABC Company shall be considered as Third Party.

Collection

Data Collection as part of the CCPA, means buying, renting, gathering, obtaining, receiving, or accessing any personal information pertaining to a consumer by any means. This includes any data collected with the direct active participation of the consumer, or data collection by means of agreements with other parties. Mere caching of data, i.e., not retaining or storing personal information, also constitutes as data collection under the CCPA. In simple terms, if you access personal information, then you are considered to be collecting personal information.

Consent

As a thumb-rule, a business may collect information without consent, and by providing a notice of collection. However, as part of CCPA compliance, a business needs to provide the ability to opt-out of sale of personal information.

A few opt-in rules apply for the consumer under the age of 16, prior to the sale of personal information. In my opinion, if your business does not sell/share personal information, then an explicit opt-in may not be required. For consumers under the age of 13, a parent or guardian must provide explicit opt-in consent. Children's Online Privacy Protection Act (COPPA) applies regarding getting parental consent. I do not discuss these specific provisions in the book. If your business engages children, it is likely that you are aware of COPPA and potentially comply with the law.

Personal Information Sale

As part of CCPA, a sales includes selling, renting, releasing, disclosing, disseminating, making available, transferring, or otherwise communicating orally, in writing, or by electronic or other means, a consumer's personal information by the business to another business or a third party for monetary or other valuable consideration.

This definition is wide. Disclosure to the service provider may be exempted. Publicly available information is also exempted from this definition as part of an amendment to CCPA signed into law.

Discrimination

The CCPA prohibits discrimination against a consumer who exercises privacy rights. However, a business may offer different prices or levels of service. But, the difference must be "reasonably related to the value provided to the consumer by the consumer's data."

Additionally, a business under the CCPA may offer financial incentives for the collection, sale, or deletion of personal information.

CCPA implementation project tasks and sub-tasks

Tasks & Sub-tasks
Kickoff
Complete CCPA applicability assessment
Evaluate CCPA consulting vendors
Evaluate Privacy Request Intake Software Vendors
Choose an external vendor
Build your own privacy request intake
Identify two intake methods
Collect Data Collection Categories
Design a survey
Send survey to internal team
Collect survey data
Create email templates with categories
Collect Data Collection Purpose by Category
Design a survey
Send survey to internal team

Collect survey data
Create email templates with purpose
Collect Data Collection Sources
Design a survey
Send survey to internal team
Collect survey data
Website Cookies
Scan website and inventory cookies used
Inventory of 3rd party cookie vendors
Create email templates with sources
Collect 3rd party categories (that you sell to)
Design a survey
Send survey to internal team
Collect survey data
Create email templates with 3rd party categories
Create a list of partners and customers
List all partners (contact info)
List all customers (contact info)
List all 3rd parties you sell data to (contact info)

Applications that store personal information
Inventory all cloud and internal apps
Identify ways to look up data by consumer
Scope of privacy APIs for service providers
Create generic amendments
Partner agreements
Customer agreements
Sold to 3rd party agreements
Website disclosures and changes
Deploy privacy request intake web form
Deploy a second method for request intake
Deploy 'Do Not Sell My Personal Info' button
Deploy disclosure banner with a link
Deploy new privacy policy
List data collection categories
List data collection purposes
List data collection sources
List sold to 3rd party categories
Communications plan

Engage partners to amend agreements
Engage customers to amend agreements
Engage sold-to-3rd parties to amend agreements
Send notices to partners
Send notices to customers
Send notices to sold-to-3rd parties
Top 20 security controls assessment
Assess data security tools vendors
Assess data lookup tools and vendors
Assess CCPA training
Audit all activities

The CCPA, amendments, and regulations

Here is a quick reference to the CCPA and its amendments.

Bill	Summary	Highlights	Status
AB 375 (Legislature A. 3., 2018)	CCPA (California Consumer Privacy Act)	▪ Privacy rights to California residents ▪ Penalties for non-compliance ▪ Private action for data exfiltration (breach)	Signed by Gov. Brown June 28, 2018

AB 25 (Legislature 2.)	CCPA employment exemption	▪ Excludes employment and job applicant information from the definition of Personal Information ▪ The exemption expires on Jan 1, 2021	Signed by Gov. Newsom Oct 11, 2019
AB 874 (Legislature C. , AB 874 CCPA)	Publicly available information exemption	▪ Excludes publicly available information from the definition of Personal Information ▪ Re-iterates that de-identified or aggregate information is not personal information	Signed by Gov. Newsom Oct 11, 2019
AB 1130 (Legislature C. , AB 1130 CCPA)	Revision of personal information for biodata & breach notification of biodata	▪ Revises personal information to include biometric data, tax ID numbers, passport numbers ▪ Clarifies notice of breach for biometric data, and instructions to authenticators upon breach	Signed by Gov. Newsom Oct 11, 2019
AB 1146 (Legislature C. , AB	Exempts vehicle info for the purpose of	▪ Exception from right to opt-out vehicle info and ownership, for	Signed by Gov. Newsom

1146 CCPA)	vehicle warranty or recall	the purpose of vehicle warranty and recall ▪ Exception from right to delete the above	Oct 11, 2019
AB 1202 (Legislature C. , AB 1202 CCPA)	Create a registry of data brokers with the AG	▪ Requires data brokers to register with California AG ▪ Requires AG to provide data broker info on a website ▪ Penalties for failure to register	Signed by Gov. Newsom Oct 11, 2019
AB 1355 (Legislature C. , AB 1355 CCPA)	Allows for differential treatment of consumer and clarifies data breach provision	▪ Nondiscrimination exception if reasonably related to the value provided ▪ Fixes a drafting error on data breach provision ▪ Disclose to consumers on specific pieces of information and the categories of information ▪ B2B exemption through Jan 1, 2021 ▪ FCRA exemption for data breach	Signed by Gov. Newsom Oct 11, 2019

AB 1564 (Legislature C. , AB 1564 CCPA)	Modifies the methods for privacy request submission	▪ Two methods (Toll-free number) requirement ▪ Online only business method	Signed by Gov. Newsom Oct 11, 2019
Chapter 20 (California A. G.)	CCPA Regulations (Draft)	▪ A draft set of regulations that govern compliance with the CCPA	California AG Oct 10, 2019

CCPA-type laws in other states

Privacy has been a hot topic among several other state legislatures. This table provides a reference to privacy laws either drafted or adopted by various state legislatures. A number of these new state laws or proposed state laws copy the structure of CCPA. All of them provide consumer privacy protection. One major variation is the area of enforcement.

State	Model	Effective Date	Rights	Likelihood of passing
Nevada	CCPA opt-out amendment	Oct 1, 2019	Opt-out	Passed
Hawaii	CCPA	Upon approval	Access, deletion, opt-out	High
Maryland	CCPA	Jan 1, 2021	Access, deletion, opt-out	High
Massachusetts	CCPA	Jan 1, 2023	Access, deletion, opt-out	Uncertain
Mississippi	CCPA	July 1, 2019	Access, deletion, opt-out	None (bill died)
New Mexico	CCPA	July 1, 2020	Access, deletion, opt-out	High
New York	CCPA (disclosure changes)	Upon approval	Access	High
North Dakota	CCPA (written consent)	Not specified	Access	Uncertain
Rhode Island	CCPA (AG rule-making)	Upon approval	Access, deletion, opt-out	High
Washington	CCPA	Upon approval	Access, deletion, opt-out	High

List of technology tool vendors by category

The CCPA compliance requires several types of technology tools. There is no silver bullet. There is no single vendor that provides one tool that fits all. I highlighted these categories because these tools will help substantially reduce your upfront and ongoing cost for CCPA compliance.

a) Privacy rights management (aka DSAR – data subject access rights, consent management)

Privacy rights management would mean managing the rights of the consumer, including the intake of privacy requests using one or multiple methods. Ability to define the workflows. Managing consent. While there are several vendors that address privacy rights management or DSAR, the following is a small list of vendors you could reference.

- OneTrust
- InfoSecEnforcer
- WireWheel
- Truyo
- TrustArc
- Jordan Lawrence
- Centrl
- Nymity

b) Privacy data tools (includes discovery, access, deletion and the like)

Privacy data tools could further be categories such as data mapping, discovery, lookup, and access. While de-identification and anonymization is also part of data tools, I decided to categorize those under security. It is not possible to fill this book with a comprehensive list of vendors. In my opinion, no single vendor provides a comprehensive data lookup & access tool. The following is a sample list of vendors to reference.

- BigID
- InfoSecEnforcer
- Centrl
- Clarip
- DataGrail
- Egnyte
- OneTrust
- ProofPoint
- GhangorCloud
- Securiti.al
- Spirion
- Veronis
- Bolden James
- Reltio

c) Security (the main area being preventing exfiltration (breach), encryption, de-identification, &anonymization)

Security is a very important element of CCPA compliance. As discussed in this book in detail, the private action potentially resulting in class-action is a serious and major concern. Security tools play a critical role in avoiding this. First, these tools help prevent data exfiltration (breach). Second, provide forensics and incident management if there is a data breach.

Most companies use DLP (data loss prevention) technology to prevent exfiltration (breach). However, most often turn off this tool in their networks because of substantial number of false-positive incidents. The following is a sample list of vendors to reference.

- SkyhighNetworks (McAfee)
- Symantec
- InfoSecEnforcer
- Forcepoint
- ProofPoint
- Digital Guardian
- Netskope
- GhangorCloud
- BitGlass
- ClearSwift
- CipherCloud
- Vaultive

- Gemalto
- Thales e-Security

d) A list of vendors providing anonymization is covered in the referenced report below. Here is a small list of free anonymization tools:

- ARX Data Anonymization Tool (ARX Data)
- Amnesia (Amnesia)
- μ-ARGUS (Mu)
- sdcMicro (sdcMicro)
- Anonimatron (Anonimatron)

e) This is a list of vendors that offer services to make a 3rd party vendor security risk assessment for **GDPR** compliance. The market is still evolving. You could engage them to extend to **CCPA** compliance.

- Process Unity
- OneTrust
- WireWheel
- Security Score Card
- IAPP.org

f) IAPP (International Association of Privacy Professionals) published a '2019 Privacy Vendor Tech Report (IAPP, 2019).' In this report, they identify several product categories:

- Assessment managers
- Consent managers
- Data mapping
- Incident response
- Privacy information manager
- Website scanning
- Activity monitoring
- Data discovery
- De-identification/pseudonymity
- Enterprise communications

Over 250 vendors are listed in this report. Here is a link (IAPP, 2019) for you to review this report.

Index

I

J-K

L

M

P

S

T

U-V

W-Z

About the Author

DV Dronamraju is on a mission to free the world of data breaches. DV has been developing security products for over 2 decades. He worked extensively with technology titans including Intel, Samsung, AT&T, Cisco, HP, NEC, Nokia, IBM, Freescale (now NXP), NTT Data, and Ericsson among others. His expertise spans security, networking, cloud, and data centers.

DV is the founder of InfoSecEnforcer. He is a startup advisor. And, he writes code. He lives in Silicon Valley with his wife and daughter. His favorite pastime is making pink cupcakes with his daughter.

Acknowledgments

This is my first book. I started with a plan that I would write each day and the manuscript would be done in a month. Far from it. Writing is hard, but I feel awesome that I completed the work. It would not have been possible without my friend and book-guru, Andreas Ramos. In one meeting, he made me realize that I am closer to my goal than I thought. Thank you, Andreas.

A very special thanks to my team at InfoSecEnforcer. Shaheem, Prafull, and Brad, thanks for sharing your enthusiasm, your experiences, and your expertise. Your feedback and discussions helped shape the recommendations and actions in this book.

Thanks to the team that helped edit, review, index, format, create a cover, and finally bringing the manuscript to life. Your help, your ability to deliver on schedule, are most valuable to get this book out.

Finally, I am grateful to my wife Anu, who despite her own busy work schedule put in extra effort to give me time. She helped me focus, encouraged me to do it right, and much more. I truly have no idea where I'd be if she hadn't given me the time needed. To my 5 year old daughter, Nimisha, thank you for letting me spend a few nights away – not reading you a book before bedtime. And, thank you for those hugs when I most needed them.